D0431317

The Seven Common Sins of Parenting an Only Child

Carolyn White

Foreword by Kirsten Smith

The Seven Common Sins of Parenting an Only Child

A Guide for Parents, Kids, and Families

JOSSEY-BASS
A Wiley Imprint
www.josseybass.com

Published by Jossey-Bass
A Wiley Imprint
989 Market Street, San Francisco, CA 94103-1741 www.josseybass.com

Jossey-Bass books and products are available through most bookstores. To contact Jossey-Bass directly call our Customer Care Department within the U.S. at 800-956-7739, outside the U.S. at 317-572-3986, or fax 317-572-4002.

Jossey-Bass also publishes its books in a variety of electronic formats. Some content that appears in print may not be available in electronic books.

Library of Congress Cataloging-in-Publication Data

White, Carolyn, date.
The seven common sins of parenting an only child : a guide for parents, kids, and families / Carolyn White ; foreword by Kirsten Smith.— 1st ed.
p. cm.
Includes bibliographical references.
ISBN 0-7879-6961-3 (alk. paper)
1. Only child. 2. Parenting. 3. Child rearing. 4. Parent and child. I. Title.
HQ777.3W45 2004
649'.142—dc22 2004000143

Printed in the United States of America
FIRST EDITION

PB Printing 10 9 8 7 6 5 4 3 2 1

Contents

Foreword

It takes one to know one. And it most definitely takes a mother of an only child to know an only child. That's how I met my neighbor Carolyn White, who pegged me immediately as an "only." Don't ask me how she knew, but I'm convinced that Carolyn has a sixth sense about only children. Once I identified myself to Carolyn as a member of The Tribe, my fate as one of her subjects was sealed. Shortly after the release of *Legally Blonde*, a movie I cowrote (and one that proudly features a strong, determined only child heroine), Carolyn interviewed me for *Only Child*, the magazine she and her husband, Chuck, publish.

When Carolyn asked me how being an only child has influenced who I am, I said that I felt I was supported and nurtured in a way that many of my peers were not. Being the sole offspring, I was encouraged by my parents to believe that I could do whatever I wanted. What I wanted came in the form of an addiction to reading, writing, and watching stories. If I had a sibling, who knows if I'd have taken this path, and who knows if it would have been supported the way my parents supported it. I feel incredibly lucky that my parents allowed me, as an only child, the time I needed to "live in my head." As for my parents, they feel incredibly lucky that I'm actually making a living at it and that I don't have to borrow money anymore!

When Carolyn and I sat down for our interview, it was clear that I was in for a very special kind of grilling. After plying me with red wine, my neighbor assumed the role of a gently cheerful, and sweetly ruthless, interrogator. She managed to unearth stories that

I never imagined telling my best friend. Happily, though, when the article was published, I didn't regret a word of it. Carolyn approaches her subjects with as much affection as she does psychological insight. When she told me she was writing a book called *The Seven Common Sins of Parenting an Only Child*, I couldn't wait to read it. I knew the book would contain not only her trademark practical advice and keen observations about only children and their parents but also an array of juicy anecdotes that only Carolyn White could unearth. After reading her book, I'm amazed to see that she has not only succeeded in her task but has exceeded my expectations. *The Seven Common Sins* is a wonderfully readable book that speaks clearly to parents and to people like me, who want to gain insights into both their past as only children and their futures as possible parents of only children.

Over the years, Carolyn and I have talked about the cultural stigma that only children bear and how the phrase "only child" is often synonymous with "spoiled" or "selfish." But in reality, we concluded one night over dinner, only children are actually defined by a constant curiosity about other people, a strong streak of confidence, and an innate independence. Because of stereotypes, as an only, you always feel slightly different from everyone else. In *her* book, Carolyn takes a positive approach to parenting only children. She helps parents celebrate the differences inherent in raising an only child and encourages them to take strength from their experience. I think that my close bond with my parents and the unique relationship we enjoy have (contrary to what people may say about only children) enhanced my capacity for sharing and increased my feelings of loyalty to people in my career and my friends and family. Thanks to them, I always felt special as a child, and I've carried that feeling as a source of empowerment throughout my life. When faced with challenges—endlessly rewriting something that doesn't need rewriting, or facing the enormous quagmire of ego and attitude that rules Hollywood—I believe that the confidence I gained as an only child is my greatest weapon. *The Seven Common Sins* helps the reader understand not only how to empower their offspring but also how to empower themselves as parents.

Having met Carolyn and Chuck's daughter, Alexis, a brilliant young woman with integrity, humor, kindness, generosity, and grace, I can say with all assuredness that following Carolyn's advice can have wonderful results. And when I have my own only child, *The Seven Common Sins of Parenting an Only Child* will be my guide.

Kirsten Smith, cowriter of
the films *Legally Blonde* and
Ten Things I Hate About You
Los Angeles, California

To Alexis, who has overlooked all of my sins
and is my inspiration for everything.

To Chuck, who has always believed in me
and the power of three.

Acknowledgments

Being an effective parent of an only child takes a great deal of love and thought. Writing this book was much like that. Many wonderful people made it possible by supporting my vision, providing insights, and encouraging me to speak my mind and go the distance.

Alexis, my incredibly perceptive only child and best friend, spent many hours researching and helping me shape this book. Her faith in the project was unfailing and her creativity and point of view invaluable.

No one could have been more enthusiastic about *The Seven Common Sins* than my husband, Chuck, who started it all in the first place. He recognized the need for a no-nonsense guide that would bring together seven years of "in-the-trenches" experiences with thousands of concerned parents of only children from around the world.

Alan Rinzler, my editor and a wise only child himself, kept me on my toes, understood where I wanted to go, and helped get me there. His honesty and guidance were invaluable.

My astute agent, Joelle Delbourgo, believed in this project from the beginning and found it a good home.

I thank everyone in admissions at Crossroads School, and especially Gennifer Yoshimaru, for providing good advice, giving me their time, being my cheerleaders, and providing the laughter. I couldn't have done it without them.

I give thanks to my incredible mother, who never felt that being a grandparent to one was less than being a grandparent to more.

And special thanks go to all of the only children and the caring parents of only children who opened up their hearts through their interviews and letters. They are the soul of this book, and their experiences will help guide and sustain others.

The Seven Common Sins of Parenting an Only Child

Introduction

Twenty-three years ago, when my husband and I were in our early thirties, our daughter was born. At that time, I was considered a late bloomer and maybe still am. Most of the girls I grew up with had kids when they were in their early twenties, so even among boomers we were considered "ancient" parents. My ob-gyn even had a clinical name for my bizarre condition, which I have conveniently forgotten. I happened to glance at that term on my chart and was astonished. Because I have forgotten almost everything I learned in eighth-grade Latin, my translation was something like "ancient crone." My god, where had the time gone? I thought I was still a fairly young woman. I caught a glimpse of myself in the examining room mirror and tried to be objective, "Well, I don't look that decrepit."

Today all of that has changed. It has become almost commonplace for women to have babies well into their forties (look at Madonna and Geena Davis), and some women have even achieved motherhood in their fifties through egg donors and surrogate moms.

Before I had thrown away the last diaper box, friends and family began asking when we planned to have another child. At the time, I didn't resent their questions because we were sure that two children were our destiny. There is an old song that goes, "We will raise a family, a boy for you, a girl for me."[1] We had our girl, and because conceiving our daughter occurred almost as soon as we decided to have children, I figured that next time around we might be lucky enough to have a boy, with whom my husband could bond over cars and mechanical gadgets. Not that I am sexist or anything, but I notice that most girls aren't all that interested in the internal combustion engine. Although I had loved being a teacher and enjoyed other people's children, I had never considered myself particularly maternal. Once my daughter arrived, however, all that changed. Like most new parents, I found her infinitely fascinating and extremely funny. She talked early and walked at eight months. She was spring-loaded, sensitive, dramatic, and seemed determined to take over the world before she could even put a coherent sentence together. As we saw it, our job was to channel all that energy in positive ways, and we thought that perhaps a brother or sister would help calm her down. But nature had other plans.

When our daughter was two, we started trying for another. That was fun but it got us nowhere except frustrated. After a year and a half of disappointment, we began fertility treatments, which, when compared with what goes on today, were almost as crude as applying leeches to my body. Ostensibly, everything was OK. I was told to go home and keep track of my temperature, and, well, you know the rest. I wasn't a very good patient and didn't like having my life regulated. Neither did my husband. We decided to back off and not worry about the fertility (witch) doctor's spells. Then, voilà, I got pregnant three times in a row! And I miscarried as many times.

Four years later, we surrendered to a higher will, which seemed infinitely stronger than our own. Sure, we spent brief moments talking about adoption, which was wildly expensive and also seemed beyond our emotional resources. It was hard to imagine having every aspect of our lives scrutinized by strangers and then waiting for years, with the real possibility of ultimately being disappointed. It was just too intimidating. After much soul-searching, we came to the conclusion that our tiny tornado would be our only child, and we would make ourselves happy with that. Letting go was a relief, but there was plenty of agonizing to follow.

So When Are You Going to Have Another?

Those family members and friends whose prying I had not minded before began to draw blood when they asked if our beautiful child was going to have an equally adorable brother or sister. I was continually hurt and shocked by their aggressive comments and hardly knew what to answer, other than giving them a medical report on the condition of my reproductive system. My daughter was in preschool, and all of her friends either had or were in the process of having brothers or sisters. Suddenly, she wanted one too. Why couldn't she have what she wanted? Surely, it couldn't be that difficult. Maybe Grandma and Grandpa could get her one; they got her everything else.

I will never forget sitting by her bed night after night for about six months and explaining, in what I thought was an age-appropriate fashion, why mommy couldn't have another baby. One night, after repeating my story for about the fifth time, my lively bundle, whose days were filled with laughter, fun, and friends, turned to me with tears in her eyes and said, "There is a hole in my heart that can never be filled." I swear that I didn't make that up. Maybe she heard the phrase on *Sesame Street* or in a story read to her at school. I don't know, but it didn't matter because all of a sudden I was choking on guilt and was close to being clinically depressed about not giving my child what she said she wanted most. It has stayed with me all these years, like one of those songs you can't get out of your head once it invades. Every once in a while, as I am falling asleep or trying to pick out a ripe avocado at the market, I can still hear that plaintive voice and see that pinched little face.

Just a few months ago, I revisited that story with my now young-adult child, who listened in an offhanded way. After I finished, my daughter looked at me for a moment, tilted her head, and said in a voice that suggested I was only slightly less gullible than the Indians who gave away Manhattan, "Oh, Mom, I only wanted what Elizabeth had. If she had a new Cabbage Patch doll (those are the ones whose faces look like moldy potatoes), I wanted one too. She had a baby sister so I wanted one. I really didn't care. You shouldn't have taken me so seriously." For the first time in my life as a mother, I wanted to take serious revenge on my own child, but all I could do was sputter, "How can you be so insensitive? You don't know how you broke my heart and the guilt I carried around with me for years after." The response I got went something like, "Can I wear your peasant blouse tomorrow?"

Obviously, what was foremost on my mind was certainly not consuming her. Once she adjusted to the inevitability of not having a sibling, she went on with her life and continued to have more fun than should be legal. Like the majority of children, who are loved and feel safe, she was much more resilient than I gave her credit for being. How could I have been so misguided? Easy. Parents of only children have infinite opportunities to project into the future, but children think short term. While we are wondering how our only child will fare in the world as an adult, he is wondering whether he can sleep over at his best friend's house this weekend or about how he can catch the garter snake he saw slithering under a hedge in the garden.

Is Our Family Strange?

When I had my child, there was very little information available about only children. All I knew was what I had heard, and what I had heard wasn't good. Only children were miserable creatures, bound to grow up to be little Dennis the Menaces, causing mayhem wherever they went. I would look at my mischievous six-year-old and think that that was what I could look forward to. On days when she was unfailingly adorable and sweet, I felt like the mommy monster, leading her innocent lamb to a life of misery as an only child. And the guilt and anxiety were fueled by a media-controlled culture that portrays the ideal family size as four, not three. In those days, I only knew one other mother who had an only child. My daughter's generation is probably the first since the Great Depression to include large numbers of only children, but I didn't happen to know the women who had them. So when situations arose that I thought related to my daughter as an only child, I would phone my friend. Sometimes her anecdotes and advice about raising one child were all the reassurance I needed.

After years of feeling like the odd family out, my husband and I were worn down, worried, and confused. Could having an only child be like having a disease? Would our beautiful daughter grow up to be a misfit? Would she be the kid other kids avoid or tease because she is "weird"? How did other parents of only children feel? How were they raising their children? What were their responses when people told them that their child would be an emotional basket case because of having no siblings? We had no idea, but we thought that someday we might start a little newsletter so that we could get in touch with other parents and share experiences. We could all be insecure together.

Only Child Is Born

For a long time, our life went in other directions, and we raised our daughter the way that most parents do, learning by doing. Then the Internet happened. By that time, our daughter was almost fifteen, and we were in the middle of daily adolescent dramas. Nonetheless we felt that we had learned a lot about raising one child, which is to say that we had learned from our mistakes. I had been an educator and a writer and had worked in private school admissions for many years. The most gratifying part of my professional life was listening both compassionately and objectively to the concerns of parents and children. But as rewarding as my career had been, I felt ready to combine my experience in education and journalism and turn it into something new.

During a conversation reminiscent of one Judy Garland and Mickey Rooney might have had when they were inspired to put on a show, my husband and I looked at each other and said, "Why don't we design a Web site and a newsletter and call them *Only Child?*" Although we weren't going to publish in a barn or a garage (like Judy and Mickey), it was definitely going to be a grassroots endeavor. I became editor in chief of a modest twelve-page newsletter. My husband was the publisher and Web designer. Things began slowly, but it soon became clear that we had hit a nerve. A few years into the project, we were receiving international unsolicited publicity, including being featured on CNN and the *NBC Nightly News with Tom Brokaw*. But most amazing were the thousands of letters and e-mails that came to onlychild.com from all over the world.

Those who wrote and e-mailed were often desperate for advice and support. Many felt guilty, stressed, and confused. Some suffered from infertility and were unable to have more than one child, whereas others had made a conscious decision to have only one. But in all cases, those who contacted us sought validation. Most of all, they wanted to know how to raise their child to be a well-adjusted person. Some parents with only children were only children themselves and enjoyed their life. They wanted us to know that perpetuating an only-child family was a positive situation for them. Some parents of only children were hounded by friends and relatives to have more kids even when they felt satisfied with the size of their families. They needed to know how to deal with the unwanted pressure and unsolicited advice.

Suddenly, we were the *Dear Abby* for parents of only children, for adolescent only children, and for adult only children. We heard from parents who had overindulged their only child by failing to set boundaries and were suffering the consequences. We also answered letters and e-mails from middle-aged "onlies," seventy-year-old onlies, and twenty-year-old onlies who wondered how they would ultimately care for aging parents. Then there were the college kids who talked about their close bond to their parents and the ups and downs of separating from them. The concerns surrounding having and being an only child were greater and more far reaching than we had ever imagined.

Our newsletter grew into a small magazine. In one of those issues, I wrote a short article on what I consider to be the seven common "sins" that most parents of only children commit. The response was overwhelming. This is not to say that parents with more than one child don't also commit those sins, but everything becomes more obvious and in some ways more crucial with one. I know that because in raising my daughter we committed every one of those sins many times and still struggle with them from time to time.

Fortunately, the sins that parents of only children commit are not usually deadly. But they absolutely can be destructive in the long run if they become part of the fabric of life. I have organized each chapter of this book around one of the seven sins. They are Overindulgence, Overprotection, Failure to Discipline, Overcompensation, Seeking Perfection, Treating Your Child like an Adult, and Overpraising. The first few sins are the ones that remove us further from the kind of love and spiritual awareness needed to raise an emotionally secure only child.

Although the media would like us to think that every family unit has a mom, dad, and two kids, the reality is totally different. In fact, only-child families are the fastest-growing family unit in this country. In the last twenty-five years, the number of only children in the United States has more than doubled. Over 20 percent of today's families are only-child families. In the 1970s, only 9.6 percent of all families in the United States had only one child. Family size is shrinking in most industrialized countries. According to the U.S. Statistics Division, the birthrate in the United States is 1.93 children per woman. With 1.13 children per woman, Spain has the lowest birthrate. Italy comes in second with 1.2 children per woman. Germany's birthrate is 1.29, and Japan's is 1.33 children per woman. France is also not replacing its population, with 1.8 children per woman. Desperate to control its exploding population, China instituted a one-child-per-family policy in the early 1970s and was able to reduce growth to 1.8 children per woman. They have recently loosened this policy somewhat so that families living in rural areas and those willing to pay higher taxes can opt to have two children. Suffice it to say, millions of families throughout the world are hungry for more information on how best to raise their only children.

This book is meant to function as a straightforward guide for today's parents, whose time and energy are often limited. For example, a parent who wonders what the consequences of overindulgence might be can turn directly to the chapter on Overindulgence, rather than having to sift through information that may not be pertinent. A sin that has been committed doesn't have to be repeated—if parents are aware of how to avoid it. My approach is practical, and much of what I have to say is based on real-life experience. I am not a sociologist or a psychologist, and this book is not meant to be a scientific or academic study. But I am a parent and educator who for years has counseled other parents throughout the world.

I have interviewed hundreds of only children and parents of only children. My articles for *Only Child* have covered everything from the relationships between single parents and their only children to helping adult only children find geriatric care managers for elderly parents. The life stories, anecdotes, and professional advice that illustrate my observations about raising an only child are meant to clarify and add dimension. Many of the stories were shared with the understanding that names and details would be altered to ensure privacy. Yet nothing has been lost in translation. I hope that these narratives will help parents understand that they are not alone and will help them feel supported in the decisions they make for their child and themselves.

All of us have committed these sins at some time while raising our children (including me). The idea is to arrive at a point where we commit them as infrequently as possible. And, yes, absolution is available through our children when they tell us how much they love us and what a good job we have done raising them. Don't worry, it can happen to you but probably not until your child is a few years past puberty. Parents who refuse to recognize their sins, however, may be destined to raise only children who are incapable of separating and living their own lives. That's serious business for which little forgiveness is available.

This book is based on long-term experience and research that I hope will be useful for you in bringing up your only child. I mean to provoke reflection and conversation. If you wish to find out more about us and our publication, *Only Child*, please visit our Web site, www.onlychild.com, and e-mail your questions or concerns to information@onlychild.com. We will do our best to answer your questions.

Carolyn White
Los Angeles, California

Chapter One

Overindulgence

I am the parent of a five-year-old son who had to be taken out of his private kindergarten last week because he caused too many problems. He didn't attend preschool because I could never bear to part with him. Also whenever we talked about sending him, he cried, and I gave in. Since he is our only child, we have not been able to resist buying him the toys he asks for or giving him as much attention as he wants. The teacher has told us that Mario's reluctance to understand that others also need their time and that blocks and books must be shared is disruptive. Now I am homeschooling Mario. I know that we need to change the way we are raising our son, but I don't know how to go about it.

When your first child is born, it's like the coming of the Messiah. I don't say this lightly, but having a child has many of the characteristics of a religious experience. A first-time parent's world is turned upside down. Suddenly, everything looks brighter, more colorful, and even more dangerous. Every act takes on new and deeper significance because each baby is a miracle and a tremendous responsibility. But who said that miracles aren't demanding?

The first glimpse of our new child awes and overwhelms us. Because we know all of our faults so well, we wonder how we can possibly do justice to such a perfect creature? We vow to change our ways, to become better people, and of course to give our child all of our devotion, time, and resources. If it will make our child happy, we will do it and then do more. So we seal the pact at birth. How often have new parents uttered the phrase, "I want to give you everything"?

This impulse to provide everything under the sun to one's child is especially keen in families where there's only one recipient of this passionate largesse. Parents who choose to have one child know from the beginning that the first child will be their only one, so why not go all the way? Parents who find out later that their first child will be their last child often feel so inadequate that they will do anything to reassure themselves, including giving their child the moon, the stars, and a Mercedes if he asks nicely enough.

When there is more than one child, parents still believe in miracles, but they know the cost. They can look at their cherubic second or third born and relive sleepless nights, colic, and tantrums along with the excitement of cautious first steps and bewitching first words.

Second and third borns have to wait their turn, play with their sister's old dollhouse, and tag along to a sibling's soccer practice. They are special and irresistible but never as wondrous to parents as the firstborn, because Disneyland never shines as brightly as it does on the first visit. This is not to say that children in larger families aren't demanding; they just learn to demand less. Their veteran parents, moreover, learn to define the limits of their own emotional, physical, and material resources pretty quickly for the sake of survival.

But parents of only children don't have to adapt; they can keep giving until it hurts so much that they no longer feel the pain. They can become gratification machines because they don't know any better. After all, they are just following their basic instincts. The problem is that they don't recognize how damaging it is to provide too much understanding, too much attention, and too much PlayStation. Many parents of only children want to give their kids everything and may ask for little in return—at first.

The two basic kinds of overindulgence that parents of only children have difficulty avoiding are material and emotional, and sometimes the two overlap. Parents who spend thousands at Toys "R" Us are often trying to make themselves, as well as their child, feel better about not having a sibling. If they have chosen to have just one child, they may feel no remorse, but if they can afford the ten-foot stuffed giraffe, they think, "Why not? We only have one." Now that is a phrase that can poison a parent's brain. Why not help Maddy tie her shoes even though she can do it herself? "We only have one, and I have the time." Why not buy Chase a pair of $150 athletic shoes? After all, "We only have one." And so it goes, until the day of reckoning when an only child thinks that she is entitled to spend $300 getting her hair straightened every month.

But let's now take a closer look at these two basic types of overindulgence.

Material Overindulgence

It's a big world out there, and let's face it, Americans like it that way. We can't seem to get enough of brontosaurus SUVs, McMansions, Big Gulps, Wal-Mart, Big Macs, and Texas-size theme parks.

The most successful mall in the country, the Mall of America in Minnesota, is also the biggest. Every new hotel in Las Vegas is larger than the ones that came before. American Express ads now proclaim that spending is the new savings. What?

If our Puritan ancestors could see us now, they might consider hopping the next ship back to England. This isn't what they had in mind when they left the corruption and excesses of Europe for the New World. Their ideal was a community of modesty, free of overindulgence. Everything from their clothing to their style of worship was pared down and minimal. Granted, that was a pretty colorless and harsh existence, but it's only taken us a few hundred years to turn into specialists in overabundance. Fully 60 percent of Americans are overweight, for example.

We are besieged with choices. When I go to the supermarket, too much is asked of me. I have to decide between at least twenty different brands of laundry soap, seven kinds of nonfat Newtons, and an array of microwave popcorn brands so vast that I can imagine the entire city of Los Angeles engulfed in the sound and delectable aroma of popping corn. Sometimes I stand in the aisles for minutes at a time, reading labels and trying to make up my mind. Finally, my brain hurts and I give in, decide that I have had it, and just grab something, anything, so that I can head for home.

Recently, I went to buy a gift for a two-year-old at Toys "R" Us. I wanted some plastic food for her play kitchen. Should I have been surprised to find that there were almost as many choices in play food and miniature laundry soap boxes as there are in my local market?

The unabashed purpose of global advertising is to make us want things we don't need and then, when we have them, to make us want something else. That way we are never truly satisfied and are always eager to buy more. We want it all, and we want it fast. The more we have, the more dissatisfied we are. The more access we have to things, the more vulnerable we are to wanting more things.

So what does this have to do with the sin of overindulging a child? Plenty! This is the culture we live in. This is what our kids see, hear, and absorb by osmosis. In order to raise a child who has a sense of reality and proportion, we need to be the child's advocates for simplicity and self-discipline, so we need to focus on what really counts. It is our duty as parents to keep our kids from being roasted on the spit of consumerism and overindulgence. It is our duty to protect them from the "need" for the latest cell phone and from the relentless hype that spews from television and films. It's natural for children to be greedy. Left to their own devices, five-year-olds would gobble up Gummi Bears until they became sick to their stomachs. As parents, it's our job to educate kids about moderation and to model how to make appropriate choices.

Discouraging Greed

We work hard, so of course we indulge ourselves now and then. Health spas, vacations, and golf rejuvenate us, but we would consider ourselves overindulgent if we did little else with our lives. Satisfying our desires is restorative, but too much indulgence can be harmful. The same can be said for indulging our only children. Gratifying them may feel good at first because it's easier, but when it becomes a habit, there is great potential for damage and disillusionment.

Overindulging an only child with material possessions comes with the territory. When there is only one child, there is naturally just more to go around. Birthdays are occasions to load up the carts at the toy store, grandparents provide trips to theme parks, and there is frequently enough money for extra clothes or the latest video game, which might not be there if there were more than one child to consider.

Some only children remember Christmas mornings when they became bored with opening mountains of presents, and they asked, "Is that all?" When kids behave that way, parents are appalled but may wonder how their child got so greedy. Overindulgence is cumulative; it doesn't happen overnight. Your child won't become a shopoholic the first time you buy her an extra Barbie. But it may happen after you buy her the Barbie Dream House, the Barbie Beauty Salon, and the Barbie Modeling Agency. You buy because you have one child and you can. Guess what? Statistics show that parents of only children spend more on their one child than most parents spend on two or three!

Children can't learn values when they are given everything, and in fact they don't want everything. What children want most is the security and love that their parents give them. Parents need to work on themselves to hold back because kids need to experience longing so they can continue to dream.

Setting Limits

There is also the temptation to use games, toys, clothes, and trips as pacifiers. One mother who grew up with very little lavishes everything on her five-year-old. Instead of giving the child limits (which is really what she craves), she lets her daughter have anything if she makes a big enough fuss. When they go to a crafts store, Zoe leaves with an armload of packages, whereas her friend, also an only child, but with a more realistic parent, must choose only one.

Zoe has no limits in or out of the store. When an adult tells her that she can't have or do something, she sticks her tongue out and says, "I don't like you." When her mother makes her a special breakfast, Zoe pushes the plate away and says, "I don't like this."

Once Zoe lay on the floor and screamed because things weren't going her way, so her grandmother knelt down, kissed her, and said, "Zoe, we love you." Grandma rewarded Zoe's aberrant behavior, therefore encouraging her to repeat it. Zoe's screams were really for guidance, not for carte blanche to behave like a creature raised by wolves.

Children want and need parents to be parents. Boundaries make them feel safe. We have all seen kids whose parents allow them to run wild in stores. Like Zoe, they beg for things. And too many moms and dads panic because they don't have the strength to say no. Giving in when your child is demanding and creating a scene can feel like a simple way out. But it's the coward's way out. If we say no in a crowded store and our child throws a fit, it's embarrassing to explain what's going on to total strangers. And if we don't explain, we have to deal with their disapproving stares, even though they may have been through the same experience if they too are parents. So we smooth things over, open our wallets, and vow to work it out later at home—maybe.

But just remember, for children immediacy is everything. Kids live in the here and now. A four-year-old who gets his way at the store doesn't have the ability to understand why you won't let him have his way again. Your adult explanation, "I only bought you that Power Ranger because I had to get home to let the cable man in and didn't have time to argue," is going to be meaningless. What your four-year-old hears is this: "I had to get home to let the cable man in, and next time we go to the store, you can pick out another Transformer." In other words, he knows that he will get what he wants next time because he has more staying power than you do. He is far too young to think this consciously, but he is sure that now there's no end to the gains he can make in the toy department. He feels his power growing while you feel yours diminishing. But don't be afraid to take control and say no. Make sure, however, that you explain your reasons for denial in terms simple enough for a young child to understand them.

Planning Strategically

You need a battle plan to deal with toy store angst and lobbying for the newest video game, Xbox, Barbie, or Thomas the Tank Engine. Parents should be clear about the kind of behavior they expect from their child when they visit a store, restaurant, or theme park, and our expectations should be stated in language that is age appropriate.

Set limits at home that are well thought out and make sense to your child and your family. Then stand behind your decisions. The child who is out of control because his father won't buy him a Razor Scooter is the child whose father didn't set forth the rules long before the family car left the garage. Children become frantic and unreasonable precisely because their parents have not known how or have not had the courage to set limits and maintain them.

By the time my daughter was three, we had a toy store rule, which went something like this: if I took her with me to buy a birthday present for one of her friends, she could also pick out one small item for herself. One item only! But I wanted her to understand that the purpose of looking at toys was to choose a gift for someone else.

We discussed what the birthday boy might like and made a list (which she couldn't yet read but kept in her head) of three possible choices. Because it was a gift from her, I wanted my daughter to participate in buying it rather than picking it out myself.

Then we wrote down three things that she wanted. Three was our magic number both for the birthday child and for her, because it was small and manageable while still allowing for choice. We always chose the birthday child's gift first, then looked for what my daughter wanted. Because we had established ground rules at home, she didn't argue with me if she found something that wasn't on our list and I said no. This made our excursions pleasant times for sharing instead of a power struggle.

When I was a kid, my parents' word was law. Negotiation was not part of our vocabulary. But in a strange way, the lack of democracy in our household made me understand who I was and where I belonged. I was the child and didn't have an adult's influence. What my parents wanted came first.

My parents were everything: attorneys, judge, and jury. I didn't always like their judgments or decrees, but I rarely tried to challenge them, at least until I was a teenager. Their authority gave me something to rebel against when I was older! But we raise our children differently now, perhaps too differently. Although it's important to listen to our children, it's irrational to let them set the agenda. There were many material things that I never received as a child because my parents couldn't afford them, so I learned to make do. I wasn't exactly Orphan Annie, but I do remember wishing hard for some things that magically appeared at birthdays and others that never did. When I got things I had waited for for so long, I felt like the heroine in a fairy tale.

At eight, I was still playing with dolls and dreamed of owning a particular baby doll, but I knew better than to lobby for it. I let my parents know that I longed for it, and finally on my birthday my grandparents gave it to me. I still remember how delighted I was. I didn't have that many dolls, so it was a dream come true. I loved that doll with all my heart long after I stopped playing with dolls on a regular basis. I wonder what our children cherish in that way? If you have one Barbie, it's more important to you than if you have ten. Two Power Rangers are treasures to be slept with (one in each hand), whereas twenty get tossed in the bottom of the toy box.

Parents of only children can use an education in withholding, which is not to say that I have not been guilty of being a marshmallow from time to time. When my daughter started preschool, her favorite toy was the Little Tikes coupe. It was one of the most popular toy vehicles at school, so she often had to wait her turn to drive around the courtyard. She begged us for one of her own. She wanted to ride the coupe whenever the mood struck her, but her tears and pathetic looks didn't move us. She pointed out that her best friend at school had just gotten the car and was joyously driving it around her driveway. According to our child, Anne's parents were wonderful, but we were ogres because we refused to buy her the car.

For two years, our daughter hoped that she would get the car for a birthday, Hanukkah, or Christmas (we celebrate both). But her wishes went unfulfilled, on purpose. Believe it or not, nineteen years later, she is still disappointed about never receiving a Little Tikes coupe, but I'm not. I'm glad that the sense of disappointment is still so sharp, because it means that she learned something about not always getting what you want. Perhaps even now, as a young adult, she has dreams about pedaling that bright red and yellow cartoon vehicle down our street. If we had given her the car, driving it at school would never have been as exotic and exciting.

We live in a country where wealth, fame, and glamour are more honored than education or good works. I doubt that will change, but none of us wants our child to grow up to be a corporate crook whose mansion is built on a foundation of stolen money. Television and films conspire against teaching our kids values, and if we allow them to pickle our children's brains, we will have few weapons against rampant materialism. Television exists to sell us and our children as much stuff as possible, even when we can't afford it or don't want it. If you watch children's programming long enough, you begin to think that the universe is actually an enormous toy store or a grocery with shelves full of nothing but sweetened cereals and chocolate chip cookies. Those ad agency folks are trained to steal a child's soul. So how can we possibly win the war against cool commercials and brand names?

Creating a Sense of Responsibility

Make your child a true part of your household by giving him specific daily responsibilities around the house. Here are some things you can do for your kid:

1. *Limit television*. This includes the number of tapes or DVDs your child watches. The less your child watches, the less influence the media will have. I actually know people who don't have cable in their homes. Imagine!

2. *Create regular chores*. These will change as your child grows and can take on more responsibilities.

- *Two-year-olds:* Help water plants, pull up small weeds in the garden, help put Cheerios and dried fruit and nuts into little plastic bags for snacks, put toys away.
- *Three- to four-year-olds:* Help brush the dog or cat, help plant flowers, help water the lawn, help make sandwiches for lunch, set the table (even though forks and knives may end up in odd places), help clear the table.
- *Five- to six-year-olds:* Help make his bed (it won't look great, but so what?), hang up his clothes, help fold clothes and put them away, help make lunch and snack for school, bring in the newspaper, help bake cookies, feed pets.
- *Older children:* Take out the garbage, empty the dishwasher, vacuum, dust furniture, fold laundry, change the cat box, walk the dog, help put away groceries.

At every age, it's important to spell out priorities and to work together as a family. Part of a weekend might be spent sprucing up the family room or organizing trash for recycling. Making your child feel invested in family life will make the child less focused on material things. John Rice, a seventy-seven-year-old only child, suffered because everyone assumed that he was spoiled because he didn't have to share with siblings. But quite the opposite was the case. "Well, my parents, God bless them, had other ideas. I had to work. I learned to scrub floors, do dishes, do the wash, dust, vacuum, and that was just the inside work. I was even taught how to iron my shirts and pants, just in case I married a woman who didn't know how to do those things. Did it pay off? My wife thinks so. I always get breakfast, she cooks the other meals, and I do the dishes. I also help with the housework. What happened to me is the best thing that could happen to an only child."

Learning How to Say No

When our child is a toddler, we don't think twice about saying no when she tries to stick her finger in a light socket or cross the street without holding our hand. As children grow and experience the world, they test us on a daily basis in other ways. Saying no because you don't want your only child to be spoiled or inconsiderate or to deprive you of your sanity is an acquired skill that you can learn as your child develops.

Of course, kids are masters at wearing us down until we give in because it seems like less trouble. After all, how much campaigning and arguing can we take? Our greatest enemy in the war against "no" is ambivalence. With fair and suitable discipline, we can teach our children values that will ultimately become part of their moral code.

But this isn't the nineteenth century, and our children aren't objects. Their feelings and needs must also be considered. This means that parents have to be thoughtful, but not so thoughtful that they become indecisive. Rules must be made and implemented before things end badly. That's a challenge, and all of us can remember times when we waffled. But satisfying your only child's whims will create a frightened, insecure person, incapable of doing without and giving to others.

Overindulged children become adults who have a tough time maintaining relationships and working cooperatively. If they always had everything growing up, they can't feel secure when they don't get it all later. We can teach our children to be effective, thoughtful people if we create an environment in which they are given clear expectations for behavior. They have to understand the consequences of their acts and how they affect others. When parents say no in a consistent and reasonable fashion, kids learn to honor those around them.

The notion that every action has a consequence is something that you can instill in your child early on. On the surface, your child may behave as if she resents the limits you set, but underneath she knows in a visceral way that when you draw that line in the sand, you are looking out for her welfare.

Almost anyone who has a young boy has felt the burn of video game fever. Perhaps your son wants a computer game that most of his friends have. The game is expensive, and from your point of view he already spends more than enough time on the computer. You don't want your son to feel left out, but you also don't want to overindulge him. If you have a partner, the two of you need to agree on how to say no. Most bright children are excellent negotiators, but your child shouldn't begin practicing law without a license before reaching puberty. You also don't want your child to pit you against each other. In unity there is strength. If your partner sees nothing wrong in buying your child another computer game, it will be hard to present a united front. Don't discuss the issue with your child until there is parental consensus.

In her book *The Answer Is No*, Cynthia Whitham reminds parents that it is their job to place reasonable limits on purchases. She suggests that if you approve of the game but can't afford it, work out a plan for your child to earn some money. If you give your child an allowance or pay him for specific work he does around the house, then agree about what he can do with that money. If you don't want him using it for video games, make that part of the plan from the start. But he won't think it's fair if you say that he can use the money for whatever he wants and then forbid him to use it for video games. It's much easier, says Whitham, to set guidelines from the beginning about what you consider appropriate. Talk with your child honestly about your feelings and listen to his. You may have different points of view, but he has to listen and give you respect. Reach a conclusion about which video games are acceptable and how much money can be spent on them. Then remind your son of that conversation if he tries later on to revise the contract.[1] You might even want to turn the oral contract into a written one. That way everything is clear.

Realizing That Less Can Be More

In 1999, Roberto Benigni won an Oscar for his film *Life Is Beautiful*. In his acceptance speech, Benigni thanked his parents for the gift of poverty. I wonder how many Americans who heard that speech understood what he was talking about. Why would anyone be grateful for poverty? Poverty is what we run from, and we hide in shame if it catches up to us. I think what Benigni meant is that poverty gave him a perspective that nothing else could. Perhaps, like my mother, Benigni believed that doing without gave him resources. He learned to make something out of very little and to draw on his creative powers. I am certainly not advocating poverty for anyone, but I do advocate a kind of manufactured scarcity, especially for only children, even when abundance is the unavoidable order of things.

Here are some examples of making do with less:

- *Make sure that your child has plenty of time to use her imagination*. My mother grew up during the Depression and had few toys. She made dolls out of cloth or sticks. Although that is extreme, she loved those makeshift toys with a fervor that I never saw my daughter or her friends feel for their dolls.
- *Encourage dramatic play*. Children from four to seven love trying on new personas. Have a box or trunk full of old clothes, hats, and jewelry that your child can dress up in. Throw in some used Halloween costumes. Boys love to dress up as Spiderman, Harry Potter, or Batman. If your little girl has seen *The Wizard of Oz*, she may enjoy acting out the part of Dorothy, especially if you can find a pair of snazzy red shoes. Then there are the old standbys: ballerinas, nurses, doctors, and karate masters.

Believe me, I know that withholding isn't easy because I have been there, but it's the only way in our consumer-driven society to help our kids learn values and keep their heads.

Emotional Overindulgence

In our home, material indulgence was rarely an issue, except with grandparents. But emotional overindulgence was a relentless force that often got the better of us. We were always there for our child, and in that respect we were good parents, but there were times when we were probably too available. We rarely disappointed our daughter, and I suppose we should be proud that we were so conscientious. But as I think back, more disappointment might have served her better. A measure of denial contributes to self-reliance, and as they get older, children need to know that they can make the right choices without us always there to prompt them. Sometimes, however, self-confident only children can actually be too responsible, and allowing them to always take the lead can be another kind of overindulgence.

Our only children need to get along with less and appreciate more, but this is not all. We have another obligation as the parents of only children, and let me say up front that this responsibility is a lot harder to fulfill than the first. Parents, grandparents, caregivers, all should take notice. Emotional overindulgence can be even more detrimental to raising a happy, healthy only child than material overindulgence. I can speak from my heart about this because it is a sin I have committed with my own child. As long as I am in the confessional here, so to speak, I will admit that when my daughter was little, I wanted to make everything smooth for her and went out of my way to do so. I learned my lesson when it became clear that she couldn't make a decision about whether to have peanut butter or tuna fish for lunch without consulting me as if I were her rabbi!

Avoiding emotional overindulgence in any form requires vigilance and sometimes the patience of a Zen master. In order to raise competent, aware children, who feel at home in the world, we need to strike a balance. We can give our children all the attention they require to feel loved without turning them into demanding potentates. Parents do not want to live with an out-of-control child, and parents should not feel guilty about keeping part of their adult life separate from their child. Setting limits and saying no can make all the difference between chaos and harmony both in your home and in your child's soul.

Psychologist Nina Asher and her husband, Steve, are the parents of seventeen-year-old Maggie. Nina says that they have always been clear about not overindulging Maggie with material things, but they have indulged Maggie's ability to be competent in the adult world, perhaps too much so. Here's how:

"We often defer to Maggie's judgment because it's good most of the time, but indulging her 'adultness' precludes us from being a separate unit. She wants to be like us, and it's often too easy to indulge that because she carries herself like an adult. But sometimes she needs help but lets things build up until she reaches meltdown because she wants to handle things on her own. For example, last year she had a problem with a math class, but instead of coming to us, she tried to work things out on her own. She carried that weight for a long time before asking us to intervene. By then, things were more serious. We need to let her know that we are there to help."

Emotional overindulgence can have consequences for parents and only children that we may not anticipate at first. But there are ways we can learn to avoid it.

Don't Sacrifice Your Life

Joan Baker is the mother of five-year-old Austin. For the first three years of Austin's life, Joan was a television producer. She decided to leave her demanding job to have more time at home with her husband and son. "I was missing so much of Austin's growing up that I changed careers so I could have a more flexible schedule."

But Joan became so thoroughly involved in Austin's life that her devotion threatened to consume her. "For a long time," she says, "we thought that Austin had to be entertained every moment, either by us or through play dates. Ultimately, I found that I was ignoring myself. I stopped going to the gym and began to feel resentful and strung out. This past winter, Austin started acting out, pushing my buttons, and I felt that I was losing control of him. I panicked and decided to get into therapy. I decided that I needed some time to myself and got my husband more involved in taking up the slack. Now, every night, I meditate for half an hour, and I don't feel guilty about telling Austin to go to his room and play with his toys.

"As a result of my pulling back, he spends long periods of time in dramatic play with his action figures and feels more secure in himself. He is much more independent. Last night, he got out of the bathtub and dried himself off before I could even get there to help him. I thought, 'Oh, I wanted to do that,' but I'm proud of him for taking that step."

Little by little, Joan is learning the difference between attentiveness and overindulgence.

Adult only children who were indulged with their parents' total attention acknowledge that it boosted their self-esteem and sense of security. But some adult only children recognize that the attention they received also carried the seeds of negative consequences.

Fran Lantz, a noted author of books for teenagers, is an only child who has an only child. On the surface, her childhood was ideal. Her parents were understanding and doted on her. But even though they didn't shower Fran with toys, they didn't necessarily follow through with discipline. Fran's mother always had time for her and in fact went out of her way to do things for Fran that she might not have done if she had had more than one child.

"I remember my mother saying no," Fran explains. "But I also remember being punished and then sidestepping it. My mother would tell me that I couldn't go outside and play with my friends, but then I'd run out when she was on the phone (sort of asking if it was OK without waiting for an answer), and I got away with that.

"A few years ago, my mother told me that when I wanted to go somewhere, she would usually drop everything and take me. At the time, I didn't know she was doing that. She was always very pleasant about it, so I didn't realize I was being indulged. She also told me, 'Your father warned me that I was spoiling you and that I would be sorry.' But for me, the biggest indulgence was my parents' attention. They always listened to me and acted like everything I had to say was interesting. They made me feel that just being me was good enough. That was great in many ways, but it had a downside. As an adult, I've had to learn again and again that nobody is impressed with me just because I'm Fran."

Assert Your Rights

Elaine and her husband, Bob, never planned on having a child at all. When their son, Mark, came along, it was a surprise that took some getting used to. Once the shock wore off, however, they were so charmed by their little imp that they had a tough time saying no to whatever he wanted, and that included sleeping in their bed long after the "family bed" had grown cold for them. Now that Mark is three years old, they long for a good night's sleep and some privacy but don't know how to go about getting it. In addition, whenever Elaine can't calm Mark down, she offers him her breast. So Mark gets what he wants while Elaine and Bob wonder how they will make it through another day without having to deal with tantrums.

The irony is that kids like Mark are actually more unhappy when they get what they want than when they don't. I agree with Wendy Mogel, who writes in *The Blessing of a Skinned Knee*, "A democratic system doesn't work well for dogs or children: it just makes them feel insecure. Parents get fooled because their children are such skilled debaters, but children are not psychologically equipped to win those debates. They don't have the maturity to regulate their own television viewing, monitor their own language, or teach themselves good manners. It's important to start teaching children that you are The Boss when they are very young, and to keep reminding them until they are old enough to leave home."[2]

So what is to be done with a three-year-old who won't sleep in his own bed? The answer isn't easy if the habit has been well established. You will have to be firm and unyielding, but this is crucial to your mental and physical health. You may need the patience of Job and the meditative ability of Gandhi. You may even get to the point where you want to call in an exorcist, but if Cynthia Whitham and I had our way, this is what you would do:

- Explain that he is getting to be a big boy, and it's time for him to sleep in his own bed.
- Don't overstimulate him before bed. Turn off the television or video. Start winding down. Have an established routine. Dinner, bath, and bed. Always make bedtime story time. Whitham suggests that you put your child in bed, read him one story, kiss him goodnight, and tell him that you will be back to check on him in a few minutes. Return a few minutes later, and if he is not asleep or is crying, tell him that you will be back again to check on him, but not if he continues carrying on like a wild thing.
- If he calls for water or another story, pretend he isn't there. When he is quiet but not asleep, return with a hug. Tell him how great he is for sleeping in his own bed. Point out that his favorite superheroes don't sleep with their mommies and daddies. Leave and then return in ten more minutes to check on him.
- If he trots out of bed, return him even if he throws a full-blown temper tantrum, complete with thrashing and screaming. If he leaves his bed again, repeat the process, over and over until he gets the message. Every time you return him to bed, say, "You're going back to bed." Don't stray from the script.[3]

Just remember, you really are bigger and stronger than your little one. You can outlast him (get earplugs if you need to), and in the end your reward will be the opportunity for intimacy with your mate (or the latest Stephen King novel). Oh, and a good night's sleep, of course.

Don't Become a Slave

Bedtime was a favorite ritual in our house, but without realizing it we also overindulged. Our daughter always slept in her own bed, but we neglected to limit the number of stories we read to her because we loved the bedtime bonding at least as much as she did. We enjoyed cuddling, kissing, and reading *Fox in Love* and *Babar* so much that we found that one story was becoming three or four. By the third story, we were usually falling asleep, and our cunning child had her eyes snugly shut. But just as we were sneaking away, her eyes would pop open, and a little determined voice would say, "Read more. Read more." Suckers that we were, we kept reading until we began to detest the adorable Madeline and would have been happy to see rascally Eloise get lost forever in the bowels of The Plaza Hotel.

Finally, we got the message. We had become the enslaved, and our five-year-old was our master. After months of this, we felt used and decided it was time to make some changes. We let our daughter know that there would be only two stories at bedtime, and when we finished those, we were leaving the room. No more snuggling. Lights out!! Well, the first week was tough on all of us. I missed the extra cuddles and the delight of kissing my daughter's forehead ten more times and smoothing her hair.

There was lots of complaining on her part. "I can't sleep. I need another story." She would turn her light on and get out of bed to find us. We firmly sent her back to her room and repeated, "No more stories. You had your two." This scenario occurred over and over for weeks. It drove us slightly nuts, but we hung on to each other, managed to stay united, and didn't cave in to the pressure. For the moment, we were repentant sinners.

Charlotte and Dan would like to repent but don't know how. Their six-year-old, Jenna, is having trouble sleeping the entire night in her own room because she is "alone and you and Daddy have each other." On more than one occasion, Charlotte and Dan have fallen for this tale of woe and have allowed Jenna to fall asleep in their room. They carry her back to bed, but she only sleeps in her room for a few hours, and then it's back to mom and dad. This couple is the victim of their daughter's clever manipulations, because they can't stand the thought that she feels "alone." Charlotte knows that two bright grown-ups shouldn't be held captive by a six-year-old, but they are willing prisoners.

They know that they are overindulging their child, but ending that behavior seems more frightening than continuing it. Charlotte and Dan probably fear being alone as well, and they are in good company. Think of the negative connotations that the word *alone* carries. We don't want to eat dinner alone, travel alone, go to the dance alone, and we certainly don't want to grow old alone. But perhaps we want to think alone, play the piano alone, pretend to be Queen Elizabeth I alone. Perhaps when we are alone, we find out who we truly are, because there are no filters through which we have to present ourselves.

Discover the Value of Solitude

Our adult lives are usually jammed with activities that almost guarantee we will never be alone. So we think it's perfectly natural to fill our child's life with dance lessons, music lessons, drama lessons, soccer, baseball, softball, Girl Scouts, and so forth. Some young children are so thoroughly scheduled that they are busy from the time they get up in the morning to the time they go to bed at night. Parents of only children feel the need to engage their children in nonstop play dates and lessons because if their child is alone, he won't know what to do with himself, and he may, heaven forbid, be lonely, which somehow connotes being an outcast.

When I was growing up, most of us didn't attend preschool; our universe was the street where we lived. After school, we played with the kids next door, and if there wasn't anyone to play with, we played by ourselves. We let our imaginations roam and lived in places where there were no limits to who or what we could be. One moment, I was a teacher and my dolls were my pupils. Then I was the star ballerina of the New York City Ballet or Snow White (my stuffed animals were the dwarves), or Cinderella. The possibilities were endless because I wasn't being rushed to lessons or play dates. Yes, I recall times when I was bored, but that was when my imagination switched into high gear.

Almost every adult only child I have interviewed or read about praises their alone time as the best thing that ever happened to them, even if there were some hours when they were lonely. A modicum of loneliness is as productive for children as it is for adults. When Henry David Thoreau went to the woods to live, he went to simplify his life and to think without the clatter of the world imposing itself on his thoughts. The writing that resulted from that experience has been influencing people to simplify their lives ever since. If Thoreau had a lot to escape from, think of all the noise that pursues us. Children also need their lives simplified so that they can sort out who they are as they transition from one stage of development to another.

The poet E. E. Cummings referred to progress as a "comfortable" disease. As a nation, we are obsessed with the next big thing, which we embrace with gusto when it comes along. Then we discard it for another big thing. But our relentless search for stimulation can, ironically, wear us out. Unlike other cultures that relax into ancient rhythms as part of daily living, we must consciously create occasions for relaxation. As that is a reality of life in twenty-first-century America, we must give our only children the opportunity to do nothing.

A taste of loneliness is something our kids can actually use. Alone time is like PlayDoh. You can twist it, stretch it, and mold it to your liking. It provides space to investigate possibilities and test the limits of imagination. Jimmy Duffy, an only child and recent University of California-Berkeley graduate, was happy to have downtime as a child. Jimmy enjoyed reading and remembers being content. There was always something he could do in his room. Sometimes he played war with his Transformers or invented sagas with his He-Man toys that went on forever.,

Actor Al Pacino enjoyed playing by himself when he was a child because in his room he was free to imitate the actors he saw in the movies without anyone passing judgment. My daughter spent days on end playing with her dollhouse and acting out soap operas with miniature people that could have assured her an hour on Oprah. Every once in a while, I would peek into her room and eavesdrop on the dramas she was crafting. She was producer, director, and cast of characters. While engaging in dramatic play, she was totally engrossed, and I can't recall her complaining to us about being lonely or bored. She relished exploring her fantasies in the safety of her own environment.

If we think that we are doing our only children a favor by indulging them with every class and play date we can orchestrate, we are wrong. Parents should seek a balance between social interaction, stimulating classes, and the opportunity for their child to pass the time alone reading, painting, drawing, or even carrying on a conversation with an imaginary playmate.

Showering our kids with material possessions and structuring their time so that they are always occupied won't teach them patience and won't help them understand that good things happen to those who can wait. If your child learns that privileges must be earned and that time spent alone will make him happy and secure in his individuality, then your life as a family is bound to be less contentious.

Because we are so success driven, it's difficult to wrap our minds around the notion that learning is the product of mistakes. I'm certain that I have learned more from my failures than from my successes. What our kids want and what they need are often quite separate, and the same can be said for us. We want to protect our only kids from disappointment, but that's not what they need. We want them to retain their innocence, but it's also our job to introduce them to the world, with all of its faults. We are our children's teachers and role models. If we can't set limits, they won't be able to either. If we are fearful and afraid to let go, they will cling to us and have trouble becoming their own people.

How Parents Can Avoid Overindulging Their Only Child

Here are some tips to help you avoid overindulging your only child:

- Don't try to give your child everything that you didn't have growing up. Your only child doesn't know what she is missing.
- Decide what your family's values are from the beginning (that would mean birth), and make them a part of your everyday life.
- Set limits that work as your child develops. Be firm but flexible.
- Allow your child to do things "wrong." Let him learn from his mistakes, as long as they don't endanger his health and well-being.
- Be good to yourself as well as to your child. Make time for you. Your child will respect you for it.
- Learn to say no and mean it. Don't let a four-year-old litigator convince you to change what you know is best for you and her.
- Teach your child the value of money by encouraging her to work, whether it's doing extra chores for you or baby-sitting for neighbors.
- As soon as your child is old enough, make sure that she gets a job. Once she understands how long it takes to earn enough money for those blond highlights, she will think twice about spending it. She will also respect how hard you work for your money.

Self-Test

Are You an Overindulgent Parent?

Test yourself and find out.

- Do you find yourself doing for your child what you know he can do for himself?
- Does your child demand attention and material things beyond what is reasonable?
- Have your child's emotional and material needs totally eclipsed your own?
- Is your child incapable of understanding the word no?
- Are you incapable of saying no because you are afraid your child will dislike you if you deny him what he wants?
- Do you have trouble setting limits for your child because you can't stand the thought of his being unhappy?

The parent of an only child who answers yes to these questions is at risk of becoming or being overindulgent. The child who knows that he can get what he wants whenever he wants it is in danger of losing touch with reality, which will negatively affect his social and emotional life. Children who get it all (or think they can) are often kids who have difficulty sharing and are actually insecure. A child who can't hear your no can't hear his teacher's no. A child who is dependent on others for encouragement can't learn to encourage himself. For the overindulged child, the glass is often half empty because there is always more out there for the taking. Pearl S. Buck once remarked that it is only the brave who should teach.

Parents must also be brave in order to keep overindulgence in check and to resist overprotection, which is a close relative of overindulgence and the problem discussed in the next chapter.

Chapter Two

Overprotection

I am a twenty-five-year-old only child who just graduated from college because I lost a couple of years along the way. My parents were tremendously overprotective and so afraid that something would happen to me that I might as well have been a prisoner. Their worries about who I hung out with, what I did, and where I went controlled them. I wasn't even allowed to get my driver's license until I went away to school. My first year of college was a disaster. All of a sudden, I had freedom, but I didn't know how to handle it. I never studied; all I did was party. I was on academic probation for two years. Then one night, I went to a frat party and drank so much that I had alcohol poisoning. Since my parents couldn't ever let go, I never learned how to handle peer pressure or make good decisions for myself. I was a mess.

The Garden of Eden was a paradise where Adam and Eve were thoroughly protected. The climate was perfect, so they didn't need clothing to shield them from heat or cold. Man and woman were in tune with each other, nature, and God. They would never know defeat or death, but neither would they know the thrill of achievement. They could do whatever they liked whenever they liked, except eat the fruit of the tree of knowledge.

Life in the garden was lush and peaceful but pretty uninteresting until the snake came along. He tempted Eve and she took the bait. How else would she have conquered her boredom? She claimed that the snake seduced her, but that's because she was ready to be seduced. Eve was as ripe for experience as the fruit she consumed was ripe for the picking. Then she sweet-talked Adam into taking a bite, but he was ready as well. Both were finished with the monotony of being looked after day and night and were ready to participate in all aspects of life. Taking the story literally, we would have to conclude that if they hadn't acted like rebellious teenagers, where would humans be? Kids have to know both joy and pain in order to grow up.

There is no mother in this tale, but if there were, she probably would have been leaning on the garden gate weeping inconsolably as her babies were tossed out into the world. From the moment our children are born, their security and safety is our primary concern. At first, our little ones are totally dependent on us, and we guard them unstintingly. But as they grow and acquire new skills, we have to open the gates ever wider, realizing that ultimately they will be able to stand on their own.

Why Only Children Are Often Overprotected

We live in a world where fear fills the air like smog. It's pumped into our homes by twenty-four-hour news programs that have no beginning or end, programs that report on all manner of distressing events: terrorist attacks, wars, codes yellow and orange, economic downturns, environmental disasters, not to mention fears caused by events occurring in our own communities and neighborhoods. These fears are especially acute for parents.

According to the U.S. Department of Justice Bureau of Justice Statistics, violent crime rates have been declining steadily since 1994 and are about to reach their lowest levels ever.[1] Yet the airwaves are jammed with horror stories about Internet predators and children who have been dragged from their homes, abused by their parents, or are struggling to make it through drug rehab. Is it any wonder that we teach our kids to defend themselves in case someone tries to grab them, warn them not to talk to strangers, and want to keep the eyes in front and in back of our heads focused on them at all times? It makes sense to be safe rather than sorry. But as much as we may want to, we can't sequester our only children behind the walls of a mythical garden to guarantee their safety. And even if we were to do that, who would they turn out to be?

Surely, all parents find themselves trying too hard to manage their child's destiny at one time or another. But only children and their parents face an unusual dilemma with regard to overprotection. Because their relationship with their child is so intimate, parents may feel that being involved in every aspect of their child's life is a natural part of their relationship. Consequently, there is a strong tendency in one-child families for parents to be overprotective. And this overprotectiveness can become a real handicap for an only child, preventing her from developing in a normal way, in a way that grows naturally from experience, from trial and error, and from the freedom to learn for herself.

Instead of being overprotective, we parents of only children need to give our child the techniques that will enable him to sort things out logically, the values that will contribute to his making sound judgments, and the self-confidence that he needs in order to know that ultimately he will be able to function competently by himself. The problem is that in order for our only children to learn what good decisions are, they have to make some bad ones as well. This is particularly trying for parents of one child to witness because so much is invested in that one individual.

Frightened parents raise frightened children, who shy away from finding their passions. I had plenty of nightmares about what might happen to my daughter when I wasn't looking or when forces more powerful than I took over. Of course, I couldn't imagine how I would ever live without her if she were taken from me. Then one day, one of those forces woke us up with a bang.

What's Out of Our Control

In 1994, Los Angeles was hit with a major earthquake. The violent shaking started at 4 A.M. My daughter was fourteen, and I remember that she, my husband, and I all clung together in the safest part of the house, while the city was being punched in the gut. The movement, the darkness, and the sounds were terrifying, but most terrifying of all was knowing that there was little my husband or I could do to protect our only child. We held on and prayed that the house wouldn't collapse. We were lucky, and all turned out well. But it was one of those moments when I realized that there was only so much we could do to shelter our child. We had sent her to an excellent school, we knew her friends and their parents, and we tried to give her the boundaries she needed to be safe under ordinary circumstances. But then there was fate—a natural disaster, an act of God, so to speak, over which we had no say.

That morning, I learned that I couldn't hold on so tightly. I had to accept the unacceptable, that something could happen to my child, but also that I would find a way to survive. Even now that my daughter is twenty-three, I worry about her driving the freeways or being caught in a horrific earthquake without us to hold on to. When those thoughts visit me, I recognize their authority and then fast-forward to something more positive. I think about the hard work my child is putting into discovering what she wants to do with her life and how far she has come since she was huddled with us on that defining morning. I have to hope that fate will be kind to us, and if not we will deal with it when we get there.

Naturally, all caring parents closely monitor their young children, but parents of only children may guard their child with particular zeal, because the child is the only one, the one who has been so difficult to conceive or to bring into the family, the one who is so precious. The parents of a single child have only that one to think about as he's hanging by his heels from the top of the slide, whereas the parents of three may have a whole lot of other things on their minds.

For example, Janet has three boys. When she takes them to the park, she knows that nine-year-old Jordan, the oldest and biggest risk taker of the three, will try to bungee-jump off the monkey bars. He is also the one who broke his leg skiing last winter and sometimes pressures his younger, more cautious siblings into following him. But then there are the other two, Cleo, who is five, and Sam, who is three. Because they are younger, they also require continuous supervision.

Because it's physically impossible to be in three places at once, something has to give. Janet has learned that she can only do her best, and she can't do more than that. Yes, there will probably be other trips to the emergency room with her little Evel Knievel, but she resigns herself to that possibility. She can only hover so much, because she has a finite amount of energy and two eyes rather than six. In addition, Janet benefits from the experience of having more than one. Her level of concern about her middle and youngest child's safety will almost always be less than she felt with her first.

When my daughter was about eight months old, my friend Tamie had two children, a son who was three and a daughter, Terry, just turning one. Terry and my Alexis began learning to walk at the same time. But when Terry fell and hit her head, Tamie barely reacted, whereas I virtually disintegrated when my child's head met the floor. I often ran after my baby to child-proof her way, but Tamie was rather casual about cushioning her child's falls, unless it looked as if she was about to crash through a glass door.

I wondered how she could be so calm, but when I asked her, she just laughed and said, "I've been through it before, and unless Terry is near something really dangerous, like the sharp edge of a table or a bottle of ammonia, I know that she will survive because her brother did. A few encounters with the floor may cause a bump or two, but eventually she will become more steady."

Sibling families have been around the block, and after the first bruise the second doesn't seem as bad, and the third barely makes an impression. Parents with multiple children know that most wounds will heal in time, but parents with one child don't quite believe it.

With their total focus on one little creature, who might have come into the world with difficulty, only-child parents are often obsessively committed to making sure that everything goes well. Even the slightest mishap can seem calamitous until they get some experience under their belt.

Real Fears Versus Real Life

Parents learn quickly that toddlers were born to be wild. One moment, they're snuggling in your lap, and the next they have managed to climb onto the kitchen counter and are using commando tactics to access a box of cookies. One minute, you are walking in your neighborhood holding your child's hand, and the next he has pulled away from you and is bolting for the street. All of your senses are on alert, your animal instincts are aroused, and then you begin blaming yourself. "Why wasn't I more careful?" "What if he had managed to open the cabinet?" "What if I hadn't caught her before she ran into the street?"

As children grow and develop, sensible parents provide opportunities for exploration and build on these in age-appropriate ways. A two-year-old can safely leave the kitchen, where you are watching her closely, and play by herself for a time in her child-proofed bedroom. You can look in on her every few minutes to make sure that everything is OK. By putting a little distance between the two of you, she establishes some independence and learns to get along without having you interact with her every minute.

In *Emotional Intelligence,* Daniel Goleman writes about Jerome Kagan, a highly respected developmental psychologist at Harvard University, who has been observing the behavior of infants and toddlers for years. In one study, a group of mothers worked to protect their shy toddler from everything upsetting, whereas another group helped their fearful child handle those moments rather than trying to avert them. "The protective belief seems to have abetted the fearfulness, probably depriving the youngsters of opportunities for learning how to overcome their fear. The 'learn to adapt' philosophy of child rearing seems to have helped fearful children become braver."[2]

Kagan also found that parents who don't rush in to save their toddlers from every upset have toddlers who learn to handle frustrations on their own. But parents who try to protect their child at every turn in an attempt to lessen anxiety actually intensify the child's stress. "In other words, the protective strategy backfires by depriving timid toddlers of the very opportunity to learn to calm themselves in the face of the unfamiliar, and so gain some mastery of their fears."[3]

The lesson for parents of only children seems clear. Loving parents protect without micromanaging. The result is a child who, little by little, learns to manage himself. The parents of an only child who can't resist removing all obstacles are more likely to raise a fearful, insecure child than are the parents who gently monitor their child.

Parents of only children don't have the benefit of being able to look back on how they dealt with the first child in order to alter their parenting behavior with the next, or perhaps to do more of the same if it was successful. Unlike families with multiple children, they can't foresee how their baby might turn out or how he will survive circumstances that are beyond their ability to direct. So they keep their gaze intently fixed and are frequently all too eager to "bubble-wrap" their child. Everything is a first time and a last time with one child, and parents can't bear anything to go wrong.

All parents are concerned about their children's well-being, but overprotective parents of only children may be unable to separate realistic from unrealistic hazards. To them, seeing their child walk alone to the park sandbox, even while they are watching, may feel as frightening as watching him run toward the ocean.

Our minds are full of what-ifs? We fear what we do not know and know that there is much to fear. Who can forget that beautiful fourteen-year-old Elizabeth Smart was snug in her bed when an intruder slit her bedroom screen with a knife and abducted her? How can we sleep secure at night knowing that a child (our child) could be so easily taken from us when we are merely in the next room? If that is the case, can any place be safe? But there is a difference between watching out for a child's welfare and becoming a smothering mother or father. All children deserve the chance to handle new experiences on their own so that they can learn about the possibilities in life and what they may or may not be capable of achieving.

Learning to Let Go

I grew up in a small East Coast town, where the worries were manageable. By the time I was eight or nine, I could leave my house on a fragrant summer morning and not be seen again until dusk. My friends and I rode our bikes everywhere. We picked blackberries growing in deserted fields, met friends for Cokes on Main Street, and even ate lunch between the crumbling headstones of the spooky Revolutionary War cemetery. We enjoyed being just a little bit scared, never had to phone home, and felt like we were pretty grown-up for a few hours. Those were idyllic days, which, sad to say, probably belong in history books. They are among my fondest memories of childhood, because they made me feel important and powerful in a way I could never feel at home. I relished those hours of being separate from my parents, and they taught me that I could begin to care for myself.

My husband and his three siblings grew up in the high desert above Los Angeles. It was *The Right Stuff* country, and most families were in the military, were scientists, or were engineers working in the space program. The family home sat on a hill with a helicopter's eye view of Edwards Air Force Base and the supersonic jets that were being tested there. Every once in a while, one of those pilots crashed. The next day, the kids would go to school and find out that someone's dad wouldn't be coming home. But my husband and his brothers were never told that they shouldn't become pilots or take risks. In fact, they took risks constantly playing in the desert. They spied on rattlesnakes, rode horses bareback, and looked for adventure in places that most adults would absolutely consider off-limits for kids. Yet they survived.

The world is less intimate now, and we aren't acquainted with everyone who lives in our towns, so perhaps a somewhat heightened vigilance is necessary. But knowing the difference between intelligent supervision and overprotection is crucial to raising a self-confident child.

I live in a big city, but I also live in a neighborhood within the city. We have always known many of the families who live around us, and we have lived on the same street for my daughter's entire life. Yet I never felt at ease letting her walk to a friend's house on her own or to our nearby shopping area, until she was in high school. Her middle school was only ten blocks from our house, and although many of the neighborhood kids rode bikes to school, we were too concerned about the traffic to let her go by herself.

As I look back, I realize that I underestimated my daughter's ability to function intelligently on her own. She knew that safety and caution were paramount, and she would never ride her bike without a helmet. If she fell off her bike and skinned a knee, there would probably be no necessity for paramedics. I was like the parent who can't differentiate between the route to the sandbox and the path to the ocean. Thinking about my daughter riding a bike to school in daylight and thinking about her walking home in the dark by herself felt the same to me. That was not realistic.

Allan and Judy Miller live in Battery Park City in downtown Manhattan. They and their only child Nathan were witnesses to 9-11 terror. Nathan's school was evacuated, but fortunately his mother worked nearby and was able to reach him quickly. Allan was in their apartment watching the madness unfold. Because cell phones were out of commission, he was unable to reach his wife and son for a number of hours. They were part of the crowd running uptown to escape. Although traumatized, the family was finally reunited at the end of the day and spent the next few months living in a hotel.

Now Judy drives Nathan to school rather than taking the subway as they did before 9-11. She is afraid that their Wall Street subway stop could be a target for terrorists. Given what this family has been through, Judy's fear is not totally unfounded. Two years later, they are back in their Battery Park City home, and life has assumed some degree of normality. Nathan, now eleven, has begun asking for more freedom, and his parents are trying to give him some.

During the day, he is allowed to walk home from a friend's house, because the path between the buildings is direct, well populated, and removed from the busy street. Soon a new soccer field will be built near their apartment, and Nathan wants to know if he will be able to walk there on his own. Allan and Judy are thinking it over. It hasn't been easy, but these parents have found a way to cope with realistic fears without subjecting their child to unrealistic ones. He has had enough to deal with, and they hope to make the rest of his childhood as normal as possible.

Tough (to Take) Love

Some parents of only children can't resist overprotecting their kids even when they are adults. For them, reality and fantasy are indistinguishable. Katia is a thirty-year-old only child whose single mother has a history of trying to safeguard her as if she were five years old. "When I went to college, she drove me and my roommates crazy with her incessant phone calls and messages," says Katia. "She asked if I was taking my vitamins, or if I had heard about the stalker who was preying on girls in another state. She wanted to know where I was and what I was doing at all times. She even made me send her my class schedule each semester. My friends jokingly suggested that I get a restraining order to keep her off the message machine." After Katia finished college, her mother tried to convince her to take a job near home in Chicago rather than in New York, so that she could look after her only daughter. Katia refused, but the phone messages have not stopped.

Love can make us do strange things, and sometimes we just love too much for our own good. Katia finally told her mother that if she didn't stop harassing her, she would change her phone number.

Building Character

If we are overprotective, how can our only child acquire character? We can't buy it for him or will it to him. In fact, the child who has everything done for him is usually less capable of handling the rough and tumble of growing up. He has no calluses, no experience at losing, few disappointments, and shallow reserves of experience on which to draw. A baby who continually wakes up at night even though he isn't hungry, wet, or ill will learn that he can make it on his own for a few hours if his parents are firm about not picking him up. As an only child grows, parents can build on that moment when they sat at the nursery door waiting for the wailing to stop. Although there is nothing they wanted more than to cuddle their child, they resisted because they knew that it would be to everyone's benefit in the long run.

Parents of only children may sometimes do their best to keep their child from the very frustrations that build coping skills. Anxiety breeds anxiety, and unfortunately it can be as contagious as the flu. If our child catches it from us, she will become far too cautious to take the risks necessary to become a secure, optimistic individual.

Amir Josephs is a twenty-seven-year-old only child whose Israeli parents brought him to live in the United States when he was a toddler. They left much of their family in Israel. Feeling disconnected, Amir's father was overprotective and had great difficulty allowing his son to forge his own identity or make the kinds of mistakes that are important learning experiences. Amir was sent to a private high school, and his father and mother had high expectations for him. But Amir was supposed to achieve those expectations within a carefully circumscribed framework.

Unlike many of his high school classmates, Amir never held a summer or after-school job, because his father thought that the jobs he could get were beneath him.

"My dad took the part of the Jewish mother," explains Amir, "but my mom was always trying to toughen me up. There were a lot of mixed messages. My dad didn't let me get a job until I was in college, because I was going to be the next president of the United States. He is a movie producer and a self-made man. He had to give up a lot to get where he is, and he didn't want me to suffer. He either did things for me or had others do them."

Amir thought that he had a good thing going until it became a bad thing. "I started to feel useless and couldn't do much for myself. That was particularly true when I had to make transitions in my life, like going off to college and then law school."

Amir's father insisted that he attend college in California, an hour and a half away from home. Although Amir had been accepted to a number of better schools in the East, his father refused to pay for them because he said that he had already paid for an expensive private secondary school education. Amir knew that was just an excuse to keep him close to home. By the time he graduated, however, Amir found a way to make a break. He applied to and was accepted to law school in England. With a British degree, he could move to Israel and practice law there, which pleased his parents.

"When I got to school in England, it was great, because I was far enough away to be independent for the first time. I could be myself," he says. "It really helped me find out who I was. I was allowed to screw up and try things I had never tried before."

Amir became more open and made lifelong friends.

"There were a lot of times when I did things that could have prevented me from getting my degree, like not showing up to class or studying for a test. But I did it, and it gave me my first real sense of accomplishment."

Deconstructing Worry

Overprotective parents try to save their child from life and tend to "overparent." Realistic parents accept their child's strengths and weaknesses and work to maximize the former and minimize the latter.

Certainly, when you are a parent, love and worry often go hand in hand. If we didn't love our children, we wouldn't worry about them. But if, like Katia's mother, we love too much, our worries can overwhelm us and harm what we value most. Psychologist Carl Pickhardt distinguishes between *constructive worry* and *destructive worry*. He considers constructive worry part of *proactive parenting*.

Constructive worry actually helps kids sort things out so that they can make good decisions. "Recognizing that a normal part of being a child is acting without always considering the risks, parents try to increase the child's vision of harmful possibilities by saying something like this, 'Because we don't want to send you blindly into a new situation you have never experienced, we want you to think about some possible problems that might arise. Then we want you to come up with some contingency plans in case any of these difficulties should occur.'"[4] Pickhardt thinks that by using this technique parents can reduce their anxiety and at the same time add to their child's confidence, enabling the child to confront new situations with enthusiasm.

Destructive worry, however, leads to compulsive overparenting. Parents who clutch their children squeeze them dry with the compulsion to organize and control. There is also something that Pickhardt calls *chain worry*. Like those chain letters we all hate, chain worry extends its nasty tentacles to include every imaginable situation. A parent who worries about a child's performance in Spanish may extend that worry to include every subject. "If you do flunk this class then maybe you'll flunk others, then maybe you'll drop out of school, and then maybe you'll end up living on the street."[5] Finding balance is crucial, but it may be elusive.

Avoiding destructive worrying is actually more important than preventing tooth decay in our children. Teeth can be fixed without too much trauma, but fixing your child's psyche is a lot more demanding. Worries should be relegated to the present, to what can be realistically managed, and not extended into the next millennium. The child who is getting a D in Spanish doesn't need to hear that he may not do well in other classes. He needs to be encouraged and mentored so that he can succeed and feel good about his accomplishment. He may be a poor language student but a whiz in math. The parent who was a strong athlete in school but has a boy whose bat rarely connects with the ball shouldn't lie awake at night wondering how to make his child the next Barry Bonds. He should either enjoy where his child is at as a ballplayer or give him opportunities to develop other talents.

Encouraging Research and Development

In order to instill self-confidence in our children, we have to start when they are very young. When your baby begins to crawl, she can separate from you in a small space that has been made physically safe. Let your child crawl until she is ready to walk, but don't push her to walk. She will get there in her own good time. Provide opportunities for "research." Encourage interaction with other infants even though it won't look like they are actually playing with one another. Give your young child time for uninterrupted play in a cognitively stimulating environment. From the time your child is old enough to understand limits, be clear and consistent about your expectations.

As our children grow, we can encourage independence step by step in ways that feel comfortable to them and to us. By taking these measures, we can avoid overprotecting our kids and can give them opportunities to grow. But first, we need to take stock of our own concerns and understand what and why they are. Although we want our kids to be aware, we don't want to infect them with our fears. You may want to do some self-analysis and ask yourself a few questions:

- Were you neglected as a child? If you were, do you confuse need with love?
- Were you mistreated in any way as a child? If you were, has it caused you to spend excessive time making sure that your child is safe?
- Has anything dangerous happened to you or your child that would lead you to be overprotective?
- If you are an only child, did your parents overprotect you? If they did, are you bringing up your child the same way without even realizing it?

Once you have a better understanding of the forces that influence you, you have a better chance of being a protector rather than an overprotector.

Give your child more freedom and responsibilities as he can handle them. If you did not feel safe as a child, chances are that you may go overboard in trying to provide an overprotected life for yours. But when you are too protective, you are telling your child that you don't believe in his abilities. Conversely, if your child knows that you trust him, he will trust himself. But don't give him too much power too early. Increase choices as he can handle them.

Some parents of only children have an instinctive understanding of how to relax supervision yet remain sensibly protective. Will and Wendi Knox are the parents of eight-year-old Landon. One summer at day camp, five-year-old Landon took on the seventy-five-foot-high rock-climbing wall. Wendi had been talking with some other parents, and Will was watching Landon. "I looked up and had to bite my lip when I saw him. I knew that he was a much more physically adventurous person than I am, and I could see that spirit as he was climbing. There was my baby, my only child, making his way to the top, but I just kept my mouth shut. I was really proud of myself."

Breaking Free

Some kids are overprotected out of necessity, which makes the transition into adulthood more difficult. Max Brooks, son of Mel Brooks and Anne Bancroft, led a rather sheltered childhood but insisted on testing himself when he got older. Max grew up in the seventies when there was a rash of kidnappings.

"I couldn't go on field trips with my class or play ball in the park with my dad," he recalls. And going out to dinner wasn't a casual event either. "During one out of every three dinners that we ate out, someone would come up to my mom or dad and ask for an autograph," he adds.

By the time Max was in college, he was more than ready to make it on his own, but his parents wanted to protect him. "My mother came to Hollywood at nineteen and had a lot of people try to take advantage of her, so she had to learn a kind of street fighting," he says. "Given what they had to handle, they couldn't understand why I insisted on experiencing adversity." Max wanted to do things on his own terms. "Let me fail," he told his doting parents. "I am going to fall on my face and learn to deal with it." This was the biggest conflict in what was an unusually close family.

When Max began his writing career, he didn't want anything handed to him. His parents offered him their beach house in Malibu so that he wouldn't have to pay rent, but he moved to an inexpensive apartment instead. He turned down their offer to help him land a writing job at *Saturday Night Live* because he didn't feel ready and was working on a different timetable. Three years later, Max was more confident about his writing talent and submitted work to the show. The producer liked what he read and hired him. After a few years of writing for the show, Max won an Emmy for his work.

Max plans to be a parent someday but doesn't intend to rescue his kids at every turn. "Maybe I'll need to be sedated," he says, "but I would love my child to make his own mistakes. I think that making mistakes without a lot of people to sweep up the mess is important." Max believes that most kids take challenges for granted. "They might not know that something is a challenge. As a kid, you see it, you meet it, and you go through it. That gives you the confidence to meet bigger challenges."

Building Confidence

You can begin instilling confidence in your child from an early age. And you can start with the most ordinary activities. Shopping either at the grocery store or the department store is an easy way to begin teaching a child some real-life skills and to begin to inspire confidence.

Design a shopping list for an easy recipe you want to make together. Then when you are at the store, have your son pick out the onions and zucchini, for example. Let him weigh the vegetables and help calculate how much a quarter of a pound of onions costs. This is a hands-on math lesson. When you get to the checkout counter, he can swipe the ATM card, and you can explain how it works (if you can). It's never too early to learn about handling money, and kids are fascinated by the debit card process. At most stores, you can watch the items line up on a screen. Kids who can read seem delighted with calling out every item and its cost.

My husband is a commercial photographer who has always had a home office. Our daughter grew up understanding what work was all about and the amount of energy it takes to get things done. We let her experience some of the conflicts inherent in running any business, and she often got to meet some of our more interesting clients. Once in a while, she accompanied my husband on shoots and even helped the assistants when she was older. This made her immensely proud and gave her a strong sense of accomplishment as well as putting her in touch with her own creativity. Our daughter saw firsthand that things don't always work out the way you thought they would and that adaptation is not only possible but invaluable.

No matter what your profession (or your partner's), you should include your child in some of what you do for a living and how you do it. By including him, you help him to learn more about you, himself, and his place in the world. If you don't expose him to what your work entails, you deprive him of access to one of the most basic elements of life.

Parents like Amir's father, who are self-made and started with nothing, can be adamant that their child will never have to experience any of the hardships they endured. They don't want their child exposed to unpleasantness, but while protecting him, they deny their child the life skills that have been so beneficial to them.

First Steps

We want our child's days to be filled with sunshine, but we must also put her in touch with some reality. The overprotected child may have to give up when things get tough. If your daughter can't play soccer as well as some of her teammates or remember her lines in a play, she may think, "I'm no good at this. Why bother?" She may blame others for her problems or expect special treatment from teachers or coaches. The parent who can't stand back, who is *too* responsible at protecting a child, may actually raise an irresponsible child who can't solve her own problems.

Try to take an objective look at your child and assess her level of responsibility and what she can handle without you or her becoming anxious. When Tanner was twelve years old, she desperately wanted to stay at home by herself without a sitter. Some friends with older siblings had been doing it since they were ten, and she had begun to feel like a baby. Tanner was a good student, had an established group of friends that her parents liked, and even did her chores without too much complaining. But Tanner's parents were reluctant to leave her by herself because they lived in an urban area and never knew who might come to the door. Although they had always encouraged Tanner's independence, she was their only child and they worried more than parents who had multiple children. They also weren't certain that Tanner was mature enough to handle an emergency should one arise. Knowing in their hearts that it was probably time to let their daughter take on this new responsibility, they talked with her and set up a plan that would give her the tools to handle staying alone, one step at a time.

At first, Tanner could stay by herself for an hour during the day after her father or the carpool dropped her off from school and her mother was still at work. The sitter could leave a little early. Tanner would have to obey the rules for staying alone that they had worked out together for her safety and her parents' peace of mind. During the hour that Tanner was by herself she was not to answer the door, even if it was the UPS delivery person. It was expected that she would follow the usual weekday rules and schedule. Once she was home, she could have a snack and start her homework. She couldn't instant-message her friends, have marathon phone conversations with them, or watch television. The truth is that if her parents weren't there they couldn't control Tanner's behavior, but they had to establish trust with her and hope that she would do the right thing. She had usually made good decisions in the past, so there was reason to think that she would continue to do so.

There were, however, even more important matters to be arranged. Tanner had to know what to do if there was a fire or if she injured herself using a knife to cut fruit for her snack. Should she answer the phone if it rang? What if the dog got sick? They discussed all these things thoroughly. Tanner's parents printed out important information, including emergency numbers and people to contact in case they couldn't be reached. They reviewed procedures for calling 911 and emphasized that she would have to provide her full name and address to the operator. The completed list was posted on the refrigerator. Tanner's parents also let their closest neighbors know about the new arrangement so that Tanner would feel comfortable asking them for help if she required it.

Tanner proved herself to be both aware and responsible. She began her homework and even called her mom at the office to check in. After a few months, everyone felt secure enough to extend Tanner's time alone at home to two hours. A year later, Tanner was able to stay by herself at night when her parents went out for the evening. She enjoyed her new freedom and for the most part didn't abuse it.

When my daughter was eleven, she and her friends began campaigning to be dropped off at the mall so that they could hang out—without grown-ups. We had gone to the mall together to see movies and shop enough times that I felt ready to let her go on her own. She was entering middle school, and it seemed appropriate to loosen the reins a bit. After all, many of her friends had already been prowling the mall by themselves for a year, and I was being conservative in granting new freedoms.

I worried that she might come into contact with kids who might be a poor influence. If I didn't let her move on, her friends would think she was a dork, but I also didn't want her to be pressured by other kids. At first, I wasn't sure that she would be able to make good decisions, but I knew that it was time to calm down and see if she could prove herself.

Feeling unsure, I checked with other parents to see what their rules were. This was before kids were all attached to cell phones and pagers. Along with other parents, my husband and I devised a check-in policy. We dropped the kids off at the mall, and our daughter agreed that she would find a pay phone and call us after about an hour and a half. We also specified a pickup time. We explained that if she and her friends were not waiting for us, the next time they asked to go off on their own, we would say no. My daughter usually did the right thing, which eased my mind and made it possible to take the next bigger steps into the bizarre dimension of adolescence.

The Perils of Puberty

Now my husband and I had to confront scarier, possibly even life-threatening, issues, such as riding in cars with sixteen-year-olds whose licenses weren't even laminated yet, attending rock concerts, and experimenting with drugs and alcohol. We figured that the inevitable stresses of living with a teenager would either make us stronger or kill us. We like to think of ourselves as survivors, so we decided that the latter wasn't even an option.

If we wanted to maintain a functioning relationship with our daughter, we would not only have to create boundaries but also give her more freedom. So in this new phase of her life, our anxiety about the mall expanded to include such cultural phenomena as rap, hip-hop, and mosh pits. (This is a nondictionary definition: a crowded dancing hole where concertgoers bash together to see who can survive the longest. This is often done to exhibit admiration for the bands that are playing. In the process, however, people have been known to suffer broken bones, dislocated shoulders, and even suffocation.) And we also had to worry about practices that have been going on for generations, such as pot smoking and binge drinking. We're talking about every parent's worst nightmares, the ones that make them want to keep their kids in preschool until they are at least forty.

When we first learned about mosh pits and raves (all-night dance parties where mind-numbing techno music is played continuously), we were terrified. How could we allow our daughter out at all? We thought about shrouding her in head-to-toe clothing and hiring a professional chaperone. But before we went overboard, we decided to vent our fears, and we told our daughter how terrified we were that something might happen to her.

We had to walk a fine line because if we forbade all concerts, it would have made them more attractive, and she might have decided to sneak around. By that time, the kids were driving and could have taken off anywhere while we thought they were at the library studying for that crucial test on themes in nineteenth-century American literature.

We had well-defined rules for driving. Our daughter was warned never to get into a car with a friend who had been drinking or using drugs of any kind. When she went out, we gave her cab money, and she knew that she could also call us at any time to pick her up—no questions asked, no screaming, and no finger-pointing.

Then there were the parties. We wanted her to have a good time, within limits. In order to keep a lid on things, we kept in touch with other parents at school and formed a kind of parental covey. When there was a party and our daughter insisted that the parents would be home, we called them ahead of time to corroborate. We trusted our daughter, but she was still a teenager who wanted to look cool in front of her friends. We found a way to watch over our emerging social butterfly while giving her some breathing room.

Free-floating teenage parties are scary because often they are held outdoors where there is no supervision. This provides a perfect opportunity for kids to bring in alcohol and drugs. If your child says that she is going to be at a party at a particular friend's house, make sure that she tells you if her plans change. Then call someone else to confirm. Our daughter's motto was, "If you are going to lie to your parents, just be sure that you are where you are supposed to be." Well, I suppose that's better than being missing in action.

Our goal was to try to protect without overprotecting, and we figured that the best way to do that was to be up-front with our child about our concerns. We expressed our fears, and our daughter assured us that she understood the dangers but wouldn't take any unusual risks. We could live with that (barely). Somehow it worked. She went to a few concerts and felt like she had some independence and was cool. To this day, I don't know everything that went on, and I don't want to know. But my daughter made it through high school and college physically and psychically intact. That's the goal.

Sleeping Over and Staying Up

When the subject of coed sleepovers came up, I was beside myself. Who ever heard of such a thing, especially in high school? Apparently every parent in the United States, Europe, and Asia, except for us, allowed their kids to go. I remember that scene well. My sixteen-year-old cried, cajoled, and used every argument in the book to get us to give in. The parents would be there; everyone would go to sleep (sure). What harm could come of it? The boys would sleep in one part of the very large house and the girls in another. Parents would chaperone and patrol. "Wouldn't the parents also want to sleep at some point?" we asked. "Oh, no," my daughter argued, "they will stay up all night." "But what if they get so tired, they fall asleep by accident?" I asked. "Oh, they won't," she assured me. That was the end of the conversation. I had to save my daughter from herself. The answer was no and remained no. Total protection was in order at that point.

We had strict rules about curfew, which were partially motivated by our selfish desire to ward off sleepless nights and ulcers. According to our charming, well-informed daughter, no other high school junior or senior had a curfew on weekends. "Well, too bad," we replied. "You will." We asked her what she thought a reasonable curfew might be, and she replied, "Oh, maybe two o'clock." We laughed. She branded us impossible and stomped away with smoke streaming from her ears.

After everyone calmed down, we managed to arrive at a weekend curfew of 12:30 A.M. for her junior year and 1:00 A.M. for her senior year, unless it was a prom night. If, however, she was more than five minutes late and didn't call us, she would be grounded the following weekend and the one after that. As I write this, I think that it probably sounds too simplistic, but it worked.

Our daughter knew that there were boundaries and rules that we were going to enforce, but if they were rules in which she had an investment and some say, it was easier. The rules made her feel safe and gave her something to complain about to her friends, and if she got into a tight social situation, she could always use her curfew or our rules as a defense. She also understood how important it was for us to be assured of her well-being. Like many only children, she didn't want to tarnish her relationship with us. It would be too painful for her to tear the fabric of our small, tight family.

If you try to mandate every detail of your teenager's life, you are destined to lose your sanity and see your blood pressure skyrocket. Your child will also be deprived of her opportunity to find her identity as a young adult. Talking and making agreements are essential ingredients in keeping your teenager as safe as possible. Here are some ways you can help foster independence, instill pride, and keep tabs on some of what is really happening in your adolescent's life.

General Guidelines for Protecting Your Adolescent

Never be afraid of embarrassing your child in front of his friends, because no matter what you do, including being on this earth, you are an embarrassment. Most teenagers would prefer to have been hatched. This is normal and only lasts until they are about nineteen. So hang in there and consider these general guidelines:

- Social life is a privilege, not a guaranteed right. Fun has to be earned, unlike when your child was little, and it was as much a part of life as *Sesame Street*. If you agree to rules that are designed to keep your teenager safe, those rules must be followed or the fun is over.
- Talking with other parents is an essential part of protecting your adolescent. When your son tells you that Sam's parents will let him drive to Alaska, you can burst his bubble. After all, you had dinner with Sam's parents the night before and know that he isn't allowed to take the car out of the garage (much less drive to Alaska), because last week he backed into a telephone pole.
- When your teenager has decided that you are the Bank of America, gently place his hand in his own pocket and tell him to get a job. Working promotes self-confidence and teaches kids how to get along with many different kinds of people. In addition, busy kids are less likely to get into the kind of trouble they can't get out of.
- In order to go out with friends on weekends, "tweens" and teenagers have to complete their chores. This gives them a sense of purpose and makes them feel needed. It may also make them temporarily angry, but kids who know that their contributions are important are less likely to betray your trust.

How Parents Can Avoid Overprotecting Their Only Child

Here are some tips to help you avoid overprotecting your only child:

- Make a list of your fears. Look at them as objectively as possible. Then eliminate the ones that don't make sense.
- Be cognizant of your child's true abilities at different stages of development. Give him opportunities to have adventures and opportunities to fail.
- Discuss trust with your child. Have faith that your family's value system will inform your child's decisions as he grows.
- Let your child solve some problems on his own. Don't always be there to pick up the pieces.
- Be aware of those times when it's important to let go. Then try to ease up without allowing your child to feel your fear. Let him find out how well he can manage on his own.

Self-Test

Are You an Overprotective Parent?

Test yourself and find out.

- Do you suggest solutions or offer help before your child even asks for it or needs it?
- Do you usually go out of your way to make your child's life easier even when it makes yours more difficult?
- Are you completely enmeshed in your child's daily life and worried about him most of the time?

(continued on next page)

- Do you find it impossible to stand by while your child sorts out a problem on his own?
- Do you go out of your way to keep your child from being frustrated?
- Do you find it hard to believe that your child is strong enough to make mistakes and recover from them?
- If you had your way, would you prefer to eliminate all risk from your child's life rather than helping him learn to handle risk?

If you answered yes to any of these questions, you should rethink what it means to guard your only child. Stand back and take a long look at who your child is and what his capabilities really are. Don't handicap him before he even gets started on his mission of discovery.

The next chapter will offer more clues about providing the kind of discipline that can help you and your child build in protective structures without building walls.

Chapter Three

Failure to Discipline

I'm a distraught parent of an only child. I've made all the mistakes that can be made: overprotection, running interference, avoiding discipline. Now I cry for my eleven-year-old son because he is so lonely. He is immature for his age, and when he gets around other kids his own age (or any age), he's so undisciplined and out of control, he gets on their nerves. What can I do?

If you took the test at the end of the last chapter, you may now be thinking about the extent to which you may overprotect your only child. You may even be sorting through the discipline and rules you have established not only to ensure your child's safety but to help civilize him as well.

Maybe you think that you are too rigid or too loose. Maybe you establish rules but don't follow through with them. If you are raising your child with a spouse or partner, your parenting styles may be quite different. You may have trouble agreeing on what to do with your child when she circumvents your rules. Being on the same page may be difficult if one of you tends to overlook infractions and can't stand being the bad guy, and the other is always the enforcer.

All I can say is don't be too hard on yourself. Disciplining a child of any age is a Sisyphean task. One moment, we think we have pushed the boulder to the top of the mountain, and the next moment we are falling backward and begging for help. One second, we think we have the answer, and the next second we can't imagine how incredibly dim we are, because a three-year-old has outsmarted or intimidated us.

Unfortunately, parents of only children can be the worst failures at making rules and implementing the ones they do make. The land mines are everywhere. All kids are cute, cunning, and strong, but only children are the most compelling of all—especially to their parents. When there is one child, all bets may be off, because we are so closely bound together that our hearts almost beat as one.

Only children can be so adored that parents can't stand the thought that their child might dislike them for even a moment. Disciplining or restricting an only child can feel like denying ourselves. What if we do something that makes her resent us? What if she thinks we are cruel or don't love her? Her misery is ours, and we feel it intensely, which is why it's so important to grasp what good discipline will mean in the long run.

The Importance of Limits

Instead of having discipline in place, taking the easy way out may feel like the best option. Why bother Alice about putting her toys away when it's not that much trouble for you to do it yourself? How many times have you asked your son to clear the table and then found him splayed out like a lounge lizard watching *The Simpsons* (which is forbidden)? You yell at him, shut off the TV, throw up your hands, and wind up clearing the table yourself. No big deal. That only took five minutes as opposed to ten minutes of persuading and cajoling. Psychologist Susan Newman suggests treating one child the same way you would treat four.[1] If you had multiple children and a dinner table that ended up looking like a World War III battlefield, chances are you wouldn't let things slide.

Every time we procrastinate about making rules or defining our wishes, our child suffers, because she feels less secure. Every time limits are stretched or rules allowed to wilt, parents compromise some of their ability to protect their child and provide a framework for her in which she can grow into a healthy adult. In fact, if discipline is not initiated and sustained, your only child has a better chance of developing some serious problems.

Long-Term Impact of Spoiling

Dan Kindlon, the author of *Too Much of a Good Thing*, studied 654 middle- and upper-middle-class teenagers. The girls who thought of themselves as "very spoiled" were three times more likely to have driven while drunk. Others, who thought their parents were not very strict, tended to develop eating disorders, try drugs, do poorly in school, and engage in risky sexual behavior.[2]

It makes sense. If there are few limits at home, kids feel insecure and may impose their own form of control, which can be at the root of problems like eating disorders. If parents aren't able or willing to spend the time setting limits, their child's sense of self will be compromised. So your only child may believe that engaging in unsafe activities or ignoring homework is no big deal. Who will notice and who will care?

Where there are no restraints, there is no real freedom for a child or for parents. Think of your home as a country that can't function without the rule of law. Anarchy promotes confusion and anxiety, not freedom and creativity.

Sometimes only children may act like they want to run the country because they are so tied into adults and wish to emulate them, but that is largely bravado. Secretly, they want rules to be in place and to be enforced so that they know where they stand. Only children can find plenty of friends, but parents are not as easy to find.

Only children tend to be highly verbal and articulate because they spend so much time with adults, so they may seem more mature than they really are. Just remember, when she tries to manipulate you to get her way, that she is a terrific mimic of adult speech and behavior. But even if she sounds like you, she isn't you. Don't let her scare you and don't capitulate. She is a child who lives under your roof and is fed, supported, and driven all over town—by you. The opportunities and choices she enjoys are those that you have elected to give her. Your only child is not in charge. You are. Don't be afraid to use your position wisely.

Rigidity Breeds Rebellion

Parents whose rules and discipline are unreasonable may find themselves with a rebellious child. Actress and only child Shirley Jones had a mother who expected her to do exactly what she was told when she was told. In a 1998 interview with *Only Child*, Shirley explained that she and her mother were in conflict with each other until she was about nine or ten. Her mother had specific ideas about how everything was to be done, and Shirley fought back. If her mother said the "the grass is green," Shirley would say it was brown. They never had physical battles, but there was no room for negotiation. Although Shirley disliked the limits her mother imposed, today she thinks it was probably good that she was asked to toe the line.

Those parents who can't bend are often overprotectors, who have the best intentions and who hope to guarantee a better life for their child than the one they had. They honestly believe that if they sequester their child and erect enough barriers, he will be safe from all danger. That may work for a while, until rampaging hormones take over his body and brain, and he morphs into the teenager from hell—the one who can't wait to escape from boot camp at any cost.

You Are the Parent; She Is the Child

You can mold your child's behavior without being authoritarian. Many of our more old-fashioned parents acted like dictators, so subsequent generations have done an about-face and have adopted a parenting style that emphasizes compassion, understanding, and friendship. This new style of parenting is a welcome change from the "children should be seen and not heard" philosophy. By getting to know our children as people, we build relationships that make them feel safe in asking our advice and communicating with us. That's the positive aspect. The negative is that we proudly proclaim that we are "child centered" but have difficulty defining our wishes.

We let kids lead while *we* toddle behind, hoping that they will take us in the right direction.

When adults and children forget their proper role, everyone feels lost. I can't count the number of times that I forced myself to repeat the following words while raising my only child: "I am the parent, and she is the child." In the middle of the most trying moments of child rearing, that reminder often gave me the strength I needed to hold my own in preteen arguments about makeup, clothing, and subsequent teenage confrontations about boys and parties.

Your only child may pout when you lay down rules, but he will continue to love you if he finds you to be fair on the whole. As he matures and wants more privileges, he will probably dislike you some of the time, but don't be too uneasy. Unless your discipline is unreasonable or excessive, that scorn will quickly pass. Or you can accept the fact that raising a child involves conflict no matter what you do. There will be days when you think you can't do anything right and days when you think you have it nailed.

Practically on the day she turned thirteen, my own daughter turned to me and screamed, "I hate you!" after I refused to allow her to attend a sleepover because she had not completed one of her chores on time. It felt like a knife had been driven into my heart. She had drawn blood, but instead of letting her know how devastated I was, I responded with, "You know, this is that time in your life when you are supposed to hate me. And right now, I still love you, but I don't like you much." My reaction thoroughly deflated her, and she slunk off to fold the laundry.

Single Parenting

Single parents of only children can struggle mightily with balancing love and discipline. They are doing the hardest job there is on their own and often with too little support. They are generally tightly intertwined with their child, and maintaining the boundary between being a parent and being a buddy can exhaust both parent and child.

Ali Mandelbaum is a case in point. She is a thirty-two-year-old only child, a singer, a songwriter, and an actress, who is now studying to be a cantor (a synagogue official who sings and leads the congregation in prayer). Ali's mom was a single parent who had great difficulty disciplining her hardheaded, dramatic only child. During elementary school, Ali was a good kid, who did what she was told most of the time. "If I didn't clean my room or do the dishes, my mom would take away a privilege, like watching TV. Or if I had been really stubborn and was supposed to play with a friend, then the play date would be canceled. But when I entered my early teen years, sometimes I would simply refuse to do things. I would be punished, but it didn't really stop me from doing it again. I thought, 'Cool, I'll just take the consequence.'"

On other occasions, Ali didn't give up quite so easily. If her punishment was not being able to watch a TV program that was important to her, she begged, pleaded, and cried real tears until her mother relented. "My mother couldn't stand to see me upset like that," Ali says. "I was her only child, and she had no one else to back her up. So I usually got my way."

Ali's mother was more concerned about her child being her friend than about creating structures in which Ali would be safe. A month after graduating from high school, Ali went to New York to study at the American Musical and Dramatic Academy, and that is when her mother's reluctance to upset her daughter had the most negative consequences. "I went to the conservatory," recalls Ali, "and some stuff went down that wasn't so great. I learned a lot, but it probably wasn't the best choice. I should have gone to a regular university. My mother wanted me to, but I wanted to go to that school, and that was the way it was going to be. I wish she would have said no."

Had Ali's mother taken a stand about college, she might have spared her daughter a lot of pain. Single parents of only children should periodically check in with themselves and assess their relationship with their only child. They should think about whether they have been more focused on being a friend than on being a parent. When situations arise that require firm guidance, they should make certain that they have not abandoned discipline in order to avoid confrontations and keep life pleasant on the surface.

The Impact of Divorce

Little or no discipline creates problems, but inconsistent discipline can be damaging as well. Divorced parents who share custody of an only child have an obligation to confer about discipline and make plans that will support their child's growth in the most loving, effective manner. Erica Warren's parents didn't do that, and she suffered as a result.

Erica is now twenty-five. Her parents divorced when she was still an infant. As soon as she was old enough, she divided her time between her mother and father. Her parents had no agreement about how to raise her, and their philosophy of child rearing was totally different.

Erica led a dual existence. Her mother was traditional and strict. Living with her father was a lot like living with Ozzy Osbourne. At her mother's, if she used a verb improperly, she then had to conjugate it. "If I talked back or stated an opinion when she felt it wasn't appropriate, then there were all sorts of punishments," explains Erica. "There were rules about everything." Erica's father was the exact opposite. "He was extremely liberal," continues Erica. "He felt that parents should be friends with their children. There were no boundaries, and I could do anything as long as I could convince him that there was a good reason for it. When I was with my mom, I wished that she could be more like my dad. And when I was with my dad, I wished that he could be more of an adult."

As an only child, Erica had no one to talk to about how unloved her mother's rigidity made her feel and about how her father's permissiveness frightened her. Her life was so confusing that by the time she was in middle school, she made up rules for herself so that life would have some order. She found a safe place between the extremes. While her friends in high school were partying, she was the "house mother," who made sure that no one went off the deep end. Essentially, she ended up raising herself.

Building Better Discipline

Your only child should be acquainted with life as you want it lived in your home because that will prepare him for life as it will be lived at school, with friends, and later on at work. Discipline teaches skills that are essential for social, academic, and career success. Those essential skills include

- Learning self-control
- Having good manners
- Treating others with kindness and consideration

Learning Self-Control

Without self-control, only children are in particular danger of being insufferably demanding. A large part of self-control is learning to wait one's turn and learning to restrain impulses. In Chapter One, Overindulgence, I mentioned that kids have to learn that patience brings rewards. In sibling families, children wait because they have to. They rarely like it, but they quickly see that someone else's needs may take precedence over theirs. If mom or dad is busy changing the baby's diapers, four-year-old June will have to wait for her glass of juice. She may whine, but mom can't change the baby and pour juice simultaneously. June can see that as a tangible fact. If an only child asks for juice, she will probably get it almost immediately because there isn't another little one waiting in the wings. The only child knows that she comes first, but parents must teach her that it won't always be that way. She may be first today, second tomorrow, and last the day after.

Babies require a lot of instant gratification, but with older children a little goes a long way. If it becomes habitual, your child will carry those expectations with him outside your home. In preschool, that "gratified" only child will be the one who absolutely must get the teacher's attention right away or who shouts out in circle time because he has to be heard immediately. The child with limited impulse control may also have trouble integrating with other kids. If he can't take a few moments to assess a situation before charging in, it's likely that the other kids will ignore or reject him. But if he can wait and observe what others are doing and play what they are playing for a while, they are more likely to take him in.

At the beginning of my life as a parent, I was the queen of gratification. I saw nothing wrong with fetching my child a snack as soon as she asked for one or with pulling Kojak the bear from under her bed the minute she whined for him. I was available to satisfy all requests because I thought that was what good parents did. As a first- and last-time parent, I didn't know any better.

But when my daughter was five, I took a good look around and had an epiphany. Compared with many of her friends, she was unable to wait even a nanosecond for either a glass of water or a new acquaintance. When we went to the park, she was fearless and rushed into groups of kids, assuming that they would play with her. I admired her guts, but she usually ran back crying because they were engrossed in their own games and didn't want to include a newcomer. I suggested that she stand to the side and watch what they were doing first; then they might ask her to join. But most forms of waiting were foreign to her, so I had to pave the way by beginning to insist, on a daily basis, that she wait for what she wanted. The goal was to teach patience so that she would be a more pleasant person and would improve her social skills as well.

Children love to interrupt their parents' phone calls, and my only child, who was used to having our full attention, was a master at turning my every phone conversation into a battle of wills. Finally, I had to take action. I hoped to start by making it clear that she could no longer interrupt my phone calls. She thought nothing of urgently asking me for help in picking out clothes for school or in choosing a book for me to read to her when I was deep in conversation on the phone. In fact, it seemed that she deliberately waited until then to ask. Although I had repeatedly spoken to her about how angry this habit made me, I had never insisted that her behavior change—or else. My usual response was to put my hand over the receiver and say, "Not now." Those words were rather meaningless because I had never told my daughter that if she continued bothering me, she would be in big trouble. I had transformed the meaning of "Not now" into, "Hang on for one second, and I will get rid of this call to give you what you want and get you off my back."

However one day when I was on an important call, she had a "huge" problem that had to be solved immediately. I put the phone on hold and told my daughter that I was busy, and she would have to wait. She grabbed my leg and hung on like a nervous puppy while pleading, "Mommy, I need you now!" Something had to be done.

When I hung up the phone, I explained why it was important that I not be disturbed. I also made it absolutely clear that the next time she interrupted me while I was on the phone, she would be disciplined, and I spelled out the following possible consequences:

- She would not be able to watch her favorite video over the weekend.
- She would not have a play date during the weekend.
- She would not be able to sleep at her best friend's house the next time she was asked.

My daughter knew that I was serious, and she could relate to each consequence. Naturally, she crossed the line a few times, but when she did, I followed through with my discipline. After a few missed sleepovers and weekends without videos, the message was firmly conveyed and the interruptions stopped.

There were still other requests that my child expected would be fulfilled right away (not when I was on the phone though), but I no longer hopped around like a kangaroo mom to satisfy them. Instead my husband and I devised a flexible reward system to help her develop self-control:

- If her father or I were on the phone and she was quiet, we thanked her, and took her on an extra bike ride through the neighborhood.
- If she was able to wait for us to help her find a missing toy or see a painting that she had made, we read her a second story at bedtime.
- When she exhibited patience, we let her know that it helped us get our work done so that we could have more time with her. If she had been especially good at waiting, we might plan a picnic in the park or a special outing with friends to the beach.

Gradually, our daughter was able to wait longer for gratification, and she began to internalize the idea that patience is worthwhile. This was a process and none of it happened overnight, but little by little we saw a change in her expectations.

Having Good Manners

There is more to manners than chewing with your mouth closed and knowing which fork to use at dinner. It also means behaving kindly and respecting others' feelings and needs, sometimes even before our own.

Good manners include cultivating an understanding of right and wrong—that is, having morals. As we help our only child to be patient, we are also teaching him to pay attention to how his words and actions affect others and how to make thoughtful choices. A child who can stop and ask himself if his behavior will make someone either upset or happy is a child who has self-control.

Raising a respectful only child requires extra resolve because we let our only children speak their minds so freely and listen so attentively to them. We value their openness but often forget that they need to listen as well as talk. Only children who don't develop good listening skills may grow up believing that what they have to say is more important than what anyone else has to say. Even though we may enjoy listening to our only child (hard not to do when there is only one), they should hear us as well. The child who continually interrupts adults or always has to draw attention to himself is a child who isn't thinking enough about those around him.

Leslie Wolf is a ten-year-old only child brimming with determination but short on manners. At school, she does well academically, but she is overzealous with her teachers and frequently interrupts them when they are presenting a lesson. If Leslie has a question, it has to be answered immediately. Her thirst for attention has turned her into something of a class joke, and her teachers are fed up with her lack of respect. Their reports home to Leslie's parents reflect this dissatisfaction. With her friends, Leslie tends to be outspoken. Other kids are attracted to her energy and boldness until she inadvertently hurts their feelings because she doesn't think before she speaks.

At home, Leslie has always been allowed to express herself in adult conversations. She feels it is her God-given right to interrupt and even talk back, because her parents don't stop her. There are no other children to compete with, so she always has the floor. Leslie's parents have never given her a clear understanding of manners and social mores. Her insensitivity has lost her friends and could compromise her social life and relationships with teachers. In the long run, Leslie's intense nature can be a valuable quality if she finds ways to channel it constructively. But she can't do it alone. Leslie's parents have to help her gain control. The ultimate goal in disciplining your child should be for her to develop an internal compass that points her in the right direction when you aren't there to monitor her behavior.

Treating Others with Kindness and Consideration

Gabe is an only child who started first grade in a new school this year. The transition has been difficult because he doesn't know anyone in his class. At home, he has been allowed to talk back to his parents, who are always trying to "reason" with him, and he is used to being in control with his friends. Unfortunately, the kids in

Gabe's new class don't welcome his relentless attempts to organize them, and his teacher has spoken to him several times about his calling other children names. The other kids leave him out of their play, and he is angry at them, but no one has taught him how to use his words properly to express his feelings. At home, Gabe's parents have not been getting along and have been insulting each other. Gabe hears it all, and because his parents are his only role models, he has adopted their behavior.

It is naive of us to think that when we are self-centered and self-serving, our only children don't see and hear everything we do. In households with more than one child, kids aren't as involved in their parents' every move. But in a one-child home, little goes unheard or unseen.

This means that we have to carefully model the behavior we expect from our child. If we want him to be fair and respectful, we can't scream "jerk" at the basketball referee who calls a foul against him. We can't drive through town raging at other drivers, and we have to be good listeners and friends. If we exhibit genuine concern for others, that is what our child will try to do as well, but we have to lead by example. When your child is rude to a teacher or another adult, take him aside and ask how he would feel if someone treated him that way. If he is mean to a friend, ask him to reflect on how he has felt when kids called him lame or stupid. Taking a moment to mull the situation over and put himself in someone else's place will usually change a child's perspective and attitude.

Only children can feel so much a part of adult life that they often think they can say anything with impunity. When you teach civility at home and let your child know that being rude or unkind won't be tolerated, he will have a better grasp of what society requires of him when he walks out your front door.

Defining Discipline

Many psychologists agree that discipline and punishment are not the same thing. Discipline should help your child achieve control over his emotions and behavior. Punishment is what happens when discipline doesn't work.

Some parents are emphatic about what discipline will be for their child, and they know how to elicit respect. "There are no treats before dinner and don't even ask." "Don't plead for candy at the market, and don't interrupt me when I'm reading. I will warn you once, and if you don't stop, you will be punished." Then they actually follow through with their threat.

If this is how you have always dealt with your child and your warnings carry weight, your child will probably obey you fairly readily in most things while he is young. But by the time he is a preteen, he is going to want explanations, and if you don't offer them, he may begin to feel that he has no control over his own life. He will argue and lobby for his position, but if you keep saying no without providing reasons, your relationship will suffer, and he won't want to confide in you.

Only-Child Discipline

Discipline isn't just about getting your only child to submit to your will. It's also about the following:

- Helping your child hear what you have to say
- Helping your child comprehend the importance of what you are saying
- Helping your child learn that rules are made for a reason and have to be followed or there are consequences

Effective, meaningful discipline includes both clear rules and conversation about them. But at some point, the conversation has to end. We should let our child know exactly what we expect, explain why, and then lay out the consequences if she doesn't comply. This is a process and the kind of discipline that is easier to practice with only children than with two or three, because our attention isn't diverted. But we don't want to be wimps. When we are finished explaining or are worn out, our child will not be emotionally scarred if we say, "Look, we aren't talking about this any longer. And if you don't stop turning on the television when I say you can't watch it, you won't be going to the park this afternoon."

Psychologist Susan Newman sees it this way: "Many parents of onlies prefer to sit down and 'talk it over.' They say, 'Now, Lisa, you must understand,' instead of saying, 'You may not speak to me that way,' or 'Daddy is busy. You will have to wait.' Having one child is often equated with having plenty of time for deep analysis of the rights and wrongs of hitting one's friend or talking back to one's grandmother. If you are tempted to adopt the 'let's talk it over' approach, remember parents with more than one are enforcing rules and laying down the law."[3]

Discipline doesn't happen overnight, and parents have to get comfortable with that. Family therapist Francine Lee finds that many of her clients with only children have trouble disciplining because they think discipline should work instantly, possibly because they expect so much from their one child to begin with.

"I tell James that he can't play computer games before his homework is finished, but I have to tell him five times, and then he fights me. Why doesn't he listen to me the first time?"

Making Clear Rules

He may not get it the first time because he doesn't understand the necessity of the rule and how it will affect him if he doesn't comply. We expect our only child to "get it" right away because we spend so much of our time "getting" them. But follow-through is essential for good discipline with an only child of any age. We can't let them railroad us with their excellent verbal and negotiating skills. Discipline doesn't just happen of its own accord. We have to see it through to the end. Here is a path to discipline that can be implemented with children of all ages. The rules and explanations will change to fit your child's age, but the format remains the same.

- *Have clearly established rules.* Your fourteen-year-old son has specified chores that he must do in order to earn weekend privileges. Those chores include emptying the dishwasher, removing miscellaneous debris from his room at least once a week, taking out the garbage, walking the dog, and feeding the cat.
- *Explain the rules.* "We can't do everything ourselves because we work hard and are tired at the end of the day. Your help is invaluable and we appreciate it. We have to work together or it will all fall apart."
- *Identify the problem.* "Sometimes these chores get done, but only after much nagging and arguing. Sometimes they don't get done at all. The cat is looking thin, the room is uninhabitable except by a special breed of cockroach, and there isn't room for one more dish in the dishwasher."
- *Provide consequences for not following the rules.* "If you can't show us responsibility at home, how can we know that you will be responsible with your friends? So it looks like you will be staying home every weekend this month."

Ten-year-old only child Angela has been irresponsible with her homework. She misplaces worksheets, forgets to do math problems, and her state report was incomplete. Angela's parents had rules about homework that were clearly spelled out. There was no television, no instant messaging, and no computer games during the week until homework was finished. But while her parents were preoccupied with some business problems, Angela took advantage of their trust, and instead of fulfilling her responsibilities, she slacked off. Angela's parents received a phone call from her teacher, who was worried about Angela's performance in school.

Although her parents were aware that they had not been able to spend as much time supervising Angela's homework as they had in the past, they had expected their daughter to fulfill her obligations. Because things were not going well, they reviewed their rules with her and restricted her privileges until she got back on track. She was not allowed to watch TV or use the computer for socializing during the week, even after homework was completed. They also required her to fill out a homework log and have it signed each day by her teacher. Until things came around, they held fast and were not persuaded by Angela's begging or attempted negotiations. Because her parents enforced the rules that were already in place, Angela came to realize that the existing boundaries were fair and that if she didn't do what was expected of her, she would lose her privileges. Swift and consistent action let Angela know that her parents were to be taken seriously.

Children Can Make Decisions

Only children should have the opportunity to make some decisions, but not the opportunity to become entitled. "Young children can and should make child-size decisions," says clinical psychologist Nina Asher. "A young child can't decide how many desserts to have in one day, but he/she can choose between ice cream and a popsicle. It is our job as parents to state clearly what the choices are and stick with them. . . . If parents set parameters in early childhood, only children will find ways to test the limits, make certain decisions on their own, and come out knowing that parents are in charge of the big picture and they are in charge of the smaller one."[4]

Rosemary is an active eight-year-old only child who is involved in a number of activities. She takes ice-skating, tennis, and ballet lessons, all of which are packed into the weekends. Now she wants to join an American Youth Soccer Organization team, and her mother has told her that if she plays soccer, she has to decide which of her activities to drop. This is an appropriate decision for a child her age to make. It would not be appropriate for her to decide how to juggle too many activities. An eight-year-old is not mature enough to handle that kind of time management. But she is old enough to know how she likes to spend her free time.

Carlos, who is twelve, and his mother had been arguing about plans for an upcoming weekend. He wanted to go to the mall with two friends and spend the day. But then he also wanted to have those friends sleep over. Mom put her foot down and said that he could do one or the other but not both. He would have to choose because he had a book report due the following week, and he was not finished with his reading. Most twelve-year-olds don't yet have a good grasp of priorities, so it's possible that left to his own devices Carlos would choose the movies, a sleepover, and throw in a trip to an amusement park for good measure.

Kids in their identity-seeking teenage years will strive for everything. But only children are especially skilled bargainers and fearless manipulators, who won't take no for an answer unless you can give them very good reasons. Teenagers should be involved in their discipline (but not their punishment) and in making larger choices, because when they own some of their discipline by helping to establish the rules, they are much more likely to follow those rules.

Jodi, a fifteen-year-old only child, who is into music like Black Sabbath, has adopted a punk rock–Goth style of dress. She has dyed her hair pitch-black, wears black nail polish and lipstick, and drives her somewhat conservative parents up a wall.

Jodi has no problems at school but enjoys pushing her parents' buttons. They dream that someday she will choose to wear blue and even listen to rap. Jodi hasn't asked to pierce anything yet, so they think that they will all live through this phase. Over the past year, their battles have mostly been about clothing and makeup. Realizing that they were getting nowhere, they have given up that fight, and Jodi can wear her Goth garb without a family war. But Jodi's parents are planning to throw a fiftieth wedding anniversary party for her grandparents, and now Jodi has to make a choice. She can either ditch the vampire look for an evening or she can stay at home.

Jodi doesn't understand why her family can't accept her for who she is. If they really loved her, they wouldn't care how she looked. Jodi's parents have explained that her grandparents certainly love her but would be offended if she showed up at the party looking like Halloween. Jodi's parents gave her a choice. She could either change her style for the party or stay home. Jodi's parents emphasized that staying home wasn't a punishment; it was an opportunity for Jodi to learn that sometimes we do things to make someone else happy, and sometimes we do things because we have to. Jodi chose to be with her grandparents. She compromised by wearing no makeup and a simple black dress. Later Jodi was also able to agree with her parents that she would continue to make family events a time to dress down. Because only children have a natural affinity for taking command, this plan worked for Jodi. She felt that she had a say in how she would dress for family gatherings, and once she made the commitment, she honored it without fighting with her parents.

Making Discipline Work with a Young Only Child

There are several important techniques that parents of only children should remember to use when disciplining their younger children.

Create House Rules

You can either raise your only child to be a cooperative member of your household or a divisive force to be reckoned with. It helps to have a set of house rules in place that you can call on if and when you run out of steam. Then you can say, "That's our rule." You might even consider giving your child some say in what those rules might be. Then, when you have to enforce them, he has a stake in things.

But in order to establish and ensure your credibility, you will have to enforce the rules without backing out. Here are some rules that a young child can understand and that you can implement comfortably:

- Clothes for school must be chosen the night before. This eliminates early-morning tears and squabbles.
- Dinnertime is family time. No television.
- There's no television on weekdays because that's when we do our homework, read, or play games together.
- Toys must be put away before leaving for a play date, or the play date will be canceled.
- There is no painting or drawing in the living room.
- Backpacks must be prepared in the evening, so we aren't late for school.

If these house rules are broken, there should be reasonable consequences. Time-outs work with some kids, and the general rule is one minute for every year of a child's age. For others, consequences have to take different forms, such as having a favorite toy put away or losing the right to take a trip with dad to the hardware store. With young children, these consequences should be immediate and must be limited enough in scope so that kids can grasp them.

In every case, of course, the punishment has to fit the crime. If your child decides to paint a Jackson Pollack-esque mural on the living room wall, you might want to cancel that trip to the beach. But if he forgets to put his homework in his backpack two nights in a row, he could lose his right to play video games over the weekend.

Offer Positive Reinforcement

The right kind of praise at the right moment can motivate kids to listen to you and do what you ask without constant prodding and arguments.

Doreen and Greg, the parents of five-year-old Milla, are frustrated by Milla's behavior in restaurants. They live in New York and often eat out because their kitchen is so small. Although they began taking Milla with them when she was still a baby, she has recently become a menace in restaurants. She wants to leave after a few minutes and begins to whimper and squirm, even though she brings toys and books with her. Doreen and Greg tried everything from threats to removing Milla from the situation, but nothing had a lasting effect.

They decided that they were going about things the wrong way. So instead of being negative, they took a positive approach. Milla loves Disney videos but isn't allowed to watch them before bed because they are too stimulating. One night, when they were at a Chinese restaurant, Milla stood up in her chair and started singing. Doreen told her that if she sat down until they were finished with dinner, she could watch part of *The Lion King* before bed. Milla was excited and quieted down. From that time on, whenever Milla behaved well in a restaurant, her parents made sure to praise her and provide a special treat, such as a Happy Meal later in the week or a ride on the merry-go-round in Central Park. A few months after they started rewarding her good behavior, Milla was able to get through a simple meal without being anxious or disruptive. This was not bribery because Milla was not being offered a treat if she behaved well. She was being given something special when she behaved well without being coaxed.

Institute a Privileges-Should-Be-Earned Policy

My four-year-old daughter liked to watch a few minutes of TV in the morning before we drove her to school. We didn't see anything wrong with that, but there were rules. If she wanted to watch *Sesame Street*, she had to dress herself and have breakfast first. We weren't going to nag, so the night before we reminded her that in order to see Big Bird, she would have to be ready for school or the deal was off. We repeated the rule for some time until it became automatic for her to arrive at the breakfast table dressed and ready.

Your four-year-old should be able to do the same. We expected our daughter to take on that small task and we made her aware from the beginning that if she didn't fulfill her part of the bargain, there would be no TV, and we stuck to it.

Focus on Problem Solving

Because they have so much clout at home, only children may prefer to set the agenda during play dates. Parents of only children frequently describe their kids as leaders, whose first instinct is to organize their friends.

Six-year-old Kyle gets so excited about dramatic play that his parents are convinced that he will grow up to be a director. When he gets together with friends, he likes to plan the action, which usually revolves around pretending to be Spiderman or Batman. Because Kyle is charismatic and has interesting ideas, his friends often choose to go along, but once in a while someone resists, there is a quarrel, and the play date disintegrates. Kids with siblings learn quickly that a brother or sister can subvert any activity, but only children may think that things will go their way forever, until friends show them otherwise.

Only children who always want to call the shots will inevitably run into conflicts with peers. When a play date ends in tears because your child has tried to dominate, you can make it a teachable moment. Don't point your finger and say, "Do you see what happens when you try to have everything your own way?"

Placing blame won't help your child alter his behavior or result in happier play. A question like that can only lead to a defensive response. Instead ask what your son thinks went wrong, because that will make him feel as if he is aiding in the process. Give him a chance to think the problem through and come up with a different approach. This will help give your only child the interpersonal skills he needs to make and keep friends. Unlike kids with siblings, who have to make compromises twenty-four hours a day, only children don't have the opportunity to problem solve, share, and say, "I'm sorry," except with their friends.

Encourage your child to consider others' feelings and what he thinks would be enjoyable for them. The next time he wants to be a superhero, but his friend wants to build with Legos, he may very well let his friend lead the way. You can help your child learn that if he is flexible and responds to what other kids want to do, he will have more fun. He may also discover that once he gives up control, the other kids will let him take the lead again when they are ready to do something different.

Making Discipline Work with a Preadolescent Only Child

If you have well-thought-out rules in place and have been consistent about enforcing them, by the time your child is older, she will know that you aren't her pawn and are serious about having her make choices and gain self-control.

Create a Consistent Schedule

Children from ages nine to twelve should have a weekday schedule that remains fairly constant. There may be soccer practice after school, for example, then home for a snack, homework, dinner, and bed. No TV. Chores may be posted on the refrigerator or on a readily accessible calendar. In addition, your child should know what the adults in the family have to do. So your schedule should be part of the calendar as well.

Keep Using Positive Reinforcement

An older child (nine or ten) can also benefit from positive reinforcement. You may not have employed this technique for some time, thinking that it is primarily effective with little ones. But older kids also respond well to knowing that they are capable of making good choices.

Andrew had always been a fairly relaxed child. Warm and loving, he was generally respectful and gave his parents little trouble—that is, until about six months ago. Now that he is nine, his mother, Scarlett, maintains that he is definitely "preadolescent." "He says things like, 'Stay out of my room' and 'Don't touch my things.' He also shoots from the hip with comments like, 'You can't tell me what to do.'" Recently, Andrew was practicing his trombone (an instrument he chose to play). Andrew kept playing the wrong notes, and Scarlett suggested that they read the notes together. Andrew's response was, "I'll play whatever I want to play." Scarlett was mortified and at a loss. Much of her discipline had relied on trying to reason with him and taking away privileges. "He tries to pick fights sometimes because it's a stalling tactic, so that he won't have to observe the rules. If we try to explain why he has to do something, he doesn't want to know the reason. Sometimes we resort to telling him that 'these are the things you have to do, and if you don't do them, these are the punishments you will receive.'"

One of her friends suggested that sometimes you get better results by rewarding good behavior than by just punishing bad behavior. Scarlett realized that although she had frequently used positive discipline with Andrew when he was younger, she had not used that tactic for a long time.

Scarlett decided to make a special calendar of the month and told Andrew that for every day he was respectful to her and his father, she would put a heart on the calendar. Once Andrew collected three days of hearts, he would get a special dessert treat. "I know that you aren't supposed to reward kids with food," admits Scarlett, "but Andrew loves desserts, and he doesn't have them that often." To her delight, the calendar worked like a charm and Andrew became his old self.

Make Them Part of the Process

Preteens want and need more independence and will fight for it. But they also need the structure that only you can provide. Pick your battles. You have to be flexible but firm. Preadolescents want to begin making some of their own decisions. Give them some opportunities to make choices.

Lena is a single parent of twelve-year-old Sari. Sari has just begun seventh grade, and her social life is blossoming. Instead of having play dates at friends' houses, Sari wants to be dropped off at the movies to meet her friends and get picked up afterward. "I give Sari some choices," says Lena. "I ask if she would like to be picked up at 7:00 P.M. or 7:30 P.M. Usually, that half hour doesn't make much difference to me on a weekend, but it makes Sari feel more in control of her destiny. If she has a sleepover, I may ask if she wants to be picked up in the morning at 10:00 or 10:30. If she also has to be at the library that day to work on a report, she will have less time to do research if she chooses 10:30. That's her decision, and she has to live with the consequences."

Making Discipline Work with an Adolescent Only Child

Discipline comes in a number of forms, and you can employ it in various combinations at different stages of your only child's development. But if preadolescence is touchy, the teenage years can be merciless and demand that parents be at their most creative when it comes to discipline.

There you are staring up at your six-foot-tall son, yelling at him to clean his room—or else. He looks down on you, smiles patronizingly, and tunes you out. Or you notice that your sixteen-year-old daughter is getting ready to leave the house in a shirt that Madonna would now consider risqué. You swallow hard and tell her to put on something more modest. She gives you a dirty look.

Although teenagers lobby for body piercings, rainbow hair color, cool cars, high-speed Internet access, and unlimited cell phone minutes, they are, in many ways, more vulnerable and tender than at any other time in their lives. Although they scream for parents to leave them alone and let them make their own decisions, that's not exactly what they mean. What they want and what they mean may change every ten minutes. What they feel in their gut is that they want to be free of you, your rules, and your demands. But if parents delve more deeply, they will find a little kid who wants to experiment but hopes that you will be there to catch him if he falls.

Only children know their parents' every weakness because they are usually very close. So it may be easier for an only-child teenager to get what he wants when he wants it than a teenager who has siblings. Be aware that your only child has all the techniques at his disposal to exploit your emotions at every turn. He is intimate with your every motivation and can read your every response.

Teenage only children should know that you are not their friend or sidekick even though they have been included in many family decisions. Much of the drama that occurs when kids become teenagers has to do with parents' inability to stand up to their child and to be clear about what is acceptable. He will want to be part of the family but not be part of the family. He will want to be there but not be there. He will complain, provoke, and test you, which is where house rules for teenagers are extremely handy.

Make House Rules Appropriate for Adolescents

House rules are important for a young child, but they become even more valuable for a teenager. Teenagers respond well to routine because their lives are so erratic. They are trying to manage rapidly changing bodies, conflicts with friends, sexual self-discovery, academic pressures, and a culture that tells them that they have to succeed before they are twenty. Everything appears designed to bend them out of shape. In order for teenagers to feel centered, they need to know that home is a safe place. But that safe place doesn't come from wishy-washy parenting. It comes from parents who can make the rules stick but who will also ask for input and who can also understand. This is a sample of the kinds of house rules an only-child teenager can respect:

- There are no after-school plans unless your child is taking music lessons, dance lessons, participating in sports, theater, and the like.
- No phone calls can be received unless they are about homework. For any other calls, parents take messages and calls can be returned when homework is completed.

- There is no television or Internet access in a child's room. Once all of his homework is completed, he may instant-message his friends fifteen minutes before bed.
- All chores must be completed before there are any social plans on the weekend. Chores may include emptying the dishwasher, feeding and walking pets, setting the table, and doing dishes and laundry.
- Agreed-upon curfews cannot be broken. But curfews can be renegotiated, depending on the social event. There are no excuses for not calling if you are going to be even five minutes late.
- No parties without parents present.

Put It in Writing

An effective disciplinary plan for a teenage only child begins with organization and with putting agreements in writing. It's hard to argue with what is in front of your face. A calendar can also work for an only-child teenager who knows how to make his parents feel guilty and sorry for him.

Any parent of an adolescent will tell you that half their time is spent quarreling about minutiae. Most only children are ready to argue cases before the Supreme Court in preschool, and you are your child's captive audience. She will bombard you with arguments such as, "If I do this, can I do that?" "Why do I have to have a curfew?" "You never let me go anywhere or do anything." "You can't tell me what to do." "Why can't you be normal?" Being prepared will help you hang on through the tornado.

Alexa, Donna and Jake's only child, had everyone running around doing her bidding. As soon as Alexa entered high school, her schedule became so complicated that she and her parents were constantly fighting about what she could and could not do. Between basketball practice, play rehearsal, homework, and an endless stream of Alexa's social activities, Donna was overwhelmed. Alexa had one version of where she was allowed to go and what she was allowed to do, and her parents had another. Donna became so rattled trying to keep everything straight that she finally resorted to a calendar. She wrote down everyone's plans on the calendar, so if there were conflicts, they were easy to spot. That made saying yes or no to Alexa's requests much easier. Alexa could see the week ahead in bold print, which allowed her to be aware of time constraints. In turn, that made Donna less likely to tell Alexa that she could do something and then suddenly remember that it wasn't possible, which always resulted in screaming arguments.

The calendar worked for all three of them. Everyone's obligations were easy to review, which prevented accusations of, "You said I could do this, and now you are telling me that I can't. What did I do to deserve this? You are so unfair."

Don't Hesitate to Punish

Dialogue is an integral part of discipline with a teenager, but sometimes your child will break the rules and behave so badly that your agreements can't be honored. In these cases, swift punishment is in order, and you should be saying, "Because I said so" or "That's how it's going to be." Don't forget that you are the parent. Don't spend more than a moment thinking about the psychic pain that you might be inflicting on your only child (who probably has a better life than you ever dreamed of having).

One of the most effective punishments is grounding, because it is immediate and nonnegotiable. It also works to limit an activity about which your child is most passionate. Meghan loves drama and recently won a large part in her school play. Unfortunately, she also "won" a C in geometry, which has convinced her mother that she is not able to balance her work in theater with her work in math. In order to keep Meghan on the right track, her mother told her that she wouldn't be able to take the lead in the play. Meghan's howls could be heard from California to New York, but her mother was firm. Until the math grade came up, the curtain was down on acting. The goal was to teach Meghan self-discipline.

If Meghan doesn't work hard, she doesn't get to play hard either. An only-child teenager's ability to have fun should be contingent on her taking responsibility. When parents insist on this equation, their child may want to dispatch them to purgatory, but at least she won't be getting away with murder.

How Parents Can Avoid Discipline Anxiety

Here are some tips to help you with your resolve to properly discipline your only child:

- Honor the difference between discipline and punishment. You don't have to punish unless discipline falls apart.
- Rules should be clear and reasonable. Make the consequences of not following rules just as clear. Your being a pushover will only make everyone miserable.
- Remember, meaningful discipline doesn't happen overnight.
- Set house rules and stick to them, unless there is a natural disaster or your child suddenly acquires the wisdom of the ancients.
- Children and parents are not created equal. We have more privileges than they do because we have earned them. They must earn theirs too.
- Reward good behavior. We all need the spiritual boost that positive reinforcement gives.
- Revise house rules as your child grows and is developmentally ready to handle new responsibilities.
- Finally, don't give in, don't give up, and don't forget that your teenager, who was abducted by aliens, will eventually be returned to you in a more recognizable form.

Self-Test

Are You a Discipline-Phobic Parent?

Test yourself and find out.

- Would you rather be sentenced to ten years of watching *Barney* than deny your child a privilege?
- Do you do your child's chores for him because you can't stand nagging him about it?
- Do you give in to pleadings for later bedtimes, curfews, and longer hours of television because you can't stand the thought of another battle?
- Are you afraid that your child will hate you if you say no one more time?
- Are you unable to set concrete rules and boundaries for your child because you're afraid of being labeled authoritarian?

If you have answered yes to these questions, then you may be a parent who is afraid of disciplining your only child. Keep in mind that the more present you are in your teenager's life and the more you put in place reasonable controls, the less he will try to oppose you. Don't lie awake at night worrying about giving ultimatums when necessary, and don't worry about losing your only child's love. You can let your child know that you won't always agree. Let him know that because you are an adult and he is a teenager, there are times when you see the world differently. But you share goals for your family and your relationship that always include love and respect.

Often discipline-phobic parents of only children are overcompensating for having only one child. Unfortunately, that guilt will drive them to ignore their child's disrespectful and controlling behavior. In the next chapter, we will focus on the guilt that leads to overcompensation and how to handle it.

Chapter Four

Overcompensation

> *I feel so guilty all the time for having one child. I feel that my son will suffer later in life. I'm not sure of why I feel this way, but I just want to do the very best for him. Most of all, I hate those stupid questions people ask, like, "When are you going to have another?" or "Aren't you worried that your son will be selfish and spoiled?"*

Material and emotional overindulgence, which were discussed in Chapter One, are motivated both by parents' inability to control their generosity toward their only child and to some degree by guilt. Many parents indulge simply because they have the means and because it feels good. They don't necessarily feel guilty for having only one child.

Overcompensation, both material and emotional, however, is entirely driven by guilt. Overindulgence and overcompensation may look like twins from the outside, but their "personalities" are different. Parents who overcompensate are always trying to make up for having an only child, but parents who overindulge may be happy with having one child and simply enjoy spoiling him.

Parents of an only child frequently respond to inner guilt, public disapproval, family pressure, and other factors with a variety of compensating behaviors that are not healthy for their child. They may try to assuage their guilt in a number of ways, from making sure that their child doesn't have to struggle for anything and making his life as seamless as possible to acting as a substitute sibling. In such common situations, parents of an only child are inclined to provide an excess of material indulgence and emotional engagement. All forms of overcompensation are on the table, because the parents will try almost anything to reduce their guilt.

Parents who have only one child because they were unable to have another often blame themselves for many things, including not adopting, not pursuing fertility treatments more aggressively, being a single parent and working long hours, and even not beginning their families earlier. The tape in their heads is all about should have, could have, would have—not a productive refrain. Parents who chose to have one child may be satisfied with their decision until the outside world lets them know that something is wrong with their family, because they "should have" more than one. At least half of the letters we receive at our publication, *Only Child,* are about guilt and about how marginalized many parents of only children are made to feel.

We have already seen that fully 20 percent of children in this country are only children, but the stigma has barely begun to fade. In fact, in smaller towns and cities parents with one child are not only thought peculiar, they are actually considered poor parents for having deprived their child of a sibling.

Here are some of the most common reasons for the guilt that plagues parents of only children and that may lead to emotional or material overcompensation:

- Parents blame themselves for having only one child.
- Two-career families, single parents, and divorced parents who share custody feel guilty about not spending enough time with their child.
- Family, friends, and even their only children make parents feel like outsiders.

Compelled by a longing to feel "normal," parents of only children strive to overcome their perceived inadequacies and may give their child too much of themselves and too many things, because they are caught in a web of unrealistic guilt.

Types of Guilt and Overcompensation

Parents of only children appear to have an endless supply of self-blame. They twist themselves out of shape trying to come to terms with what they see as one of the biggest, if not the biggest, mistake in their lives: having an only child. Mothers express this guilt freely, whereas fathers tend to be more subdued about it.

For example, Maria is the mother of a seven-year-old boy. She suffers from secondary infertility and begins every day tormented by guilt, worried that her son will be lonely and will be miserable both now and in the future because he doesn't have a sibling. She wants him "to bask" in her love and benefit from the best that she can offer financially and emotionally. Yet Maria doesn't think that will be enough to ensure her son's happiness. Instead of concentrating on giving her child an environment in which he can become his best self, she spends hours fixating on the one thing she absolutely can't give him. Adoption is out of the question because Maria's husband doesn't feel comfortable raising a child who is not biologically his own.

Here's another story: forty-six-year-old Martha and her husband waited to have kids. They were thrilled to have one, but after a few tries for a second, all of which ended in miscarriages, it's definite that they won't have any more. On the one hand, Martha enjoys being able to devote time to her nine-year-old daughter without being pulled in ten different directions. On the other hand, she gets depressed when she finds out that a friend or relative is pregnant. "Having one child seems to bother me more than it does my husband or daughter. Sometimes I feel like I am the only one on the planet who has one child. I often think that there is something wrong with me for not doing everything I can to have more children."

Here's one more example: Emma and Doug decided to stop at one child because it felt like the perfect fit for a busy, two-career couple. Doug is an art director, and Emma is a clothing designer, who owns her own company. They wanted a family but not a large one because neither wanted to compromise their careers. One child was the perfect fit, and they have been able to balance raising their daughter, Alice, with running their businesses and sustaining their creative endeavors.

They never really thought about what it meant to have an only child and were comfortable with their decision until Alice turned ten.

"Suddenly, I had pangs of guilt about depriving her of a brother or sister," says Emma. "We like our lifestyle and have just the right amount of time and money to devote to Alice and our interests. But for some reason, I started romanticizing ideas of my daughter having someone else with whom to share secrets and family stories later on in life. Maybe we have been too selfish. Doug and I are worried that our choice may be right for us but not for Alice."

Sadly, Maria, Martha, and others like them feel like damaged goods due to their inability to have more children. Parents like Emma and Doug made a carefully considered choice to have one child. Yet they too may begin to see themselves as victimizers and their child as a victim if friends and relatives criticize their decision and tell them they have done something terrible by not giving Alice a sibling. It then becomes all too easy to transfer that sense of victimization to their only child and view her as fragile and unable to cope. The truth is that only children who are raised in loving, realistic households get along with peers and adults very well. But when parents feel guilty, no matter how smoothly their family may be functioning, it's never good enough. They can't shake the feeling that they are outsiders, and they are desperate to make up for what they believe is their enormous loss.

No one ever gets everything in one family, and with the proper exposure a child like Alice will find cousins or close friends with whom she can share those family "secrets." It is certainly "romantic" to think that siblings will fill all the spaces in an only child's life. In fact, however, legions of adults with siblings can testify to the fact that as they grew older, they had little in common with their siblings and given the option might never have chosen them as friends.

Overscheduling

Overcompensation can take the form of overscheduling an only child with classes, sports, and travel in an attempt to give him every opportunity and make him the best at everything. Parents may begin to feel so bad for their child that they smother him emotionally or shower him with material things.

Danielle and Jason, for example, are the parents of eight-year-old Patti. They chose to have an only child because they can't afford another one either emotionally or financially. Although they are content with their decision, the rest of the world won't leave them alone and conspires to make them feel guilty for their choice. "People keep telling me that it's actually a sin to have just one child," she says. "Friends of mine have two and three kids and hate to spend even five minutes with them, while we enjoy spending time together as a family. I think that people should think twice before criticizing a family with one child."

Although Danielle does her best not to feel shamed by these comments, she finds herself overcompensating and wanting to "show" her critics what a wonderful child Patti is. So violin, ballet, tennis lessons, and soccer are packed into each week. Danielle feels that the time she spends cultivating Patti's interests speaks to her dedication as a parent and proves that her daughter is not a maladjusted only child but rather a talented team player. Danielle's secret hope is that Patti will become an accomplished violinist *and* a soccer player worthy of a college scholarship.

Patti chose her activities and enjoys them all, but Danielle understands that her daughter is probably overscheduled. "I know that I am overcompensating for Patti being an only child, but I just want people to know how terrific she is. Although I always want Patti to do the best for herself, sometimes I push her too much because I am overwhelmed by friends and relatives who make me feel guilty."

Excessive Emotional Protection

As we have seen, even parents who have worked hard to have a child don't give themselves much credit for making it to parenthood. Instead of patting themselves on the back for surviving painful tests, shots, failed fertility procedures, or other types of struggle and even public shame and blaming, they fault themselves for not being super reproducers. So they overcompensate by trying to make sure that their child has a life free from stress and difficulties.

For example, Ruby, an architect, and Jack, a financial analyst, fought long and hard to have their son, Craig. They endured years of fertility treatments, so when Craig made his appearance, it was something of a miracle. When their son was four, the couple decided that they wanted another child, but neither had the strength to take the fertility route again. They thought that adoption might work for them, so they attended adoption seminars and even contacted a lawyer. After assessing what it would cost to adopt and how long it might take, they concluded that the process was too complex and expensive for them to handle.

If this were a movie, the story would end with scenes of the happy threesome having fun on the beach, enjoying one another without regrets. But that's not how things have turned out. Now that Craig is seven, Ruby is awash in misgivings and guilt. She blames herself for not trying in vitro again and for not continuing with the adoption process. She regards herself as weak and cowardly and believes that she has failed her son because she has not provided him with a companion. Ruby fears that Craig will be lonely for the rest of his life, and every time she looks at him, she is convinced that he has been permanently wounded.

Jack is more grounded about it. He admits to some guilt about having abandoned the adoption program, but he has adjusted to having one child and tries to reassure his wife that Craig will grow up to be a fine person if only she will stop trying to make his life perfect. In order to feel better about having "cheated" Craig, Ruby overcompensates emotionally. She attempts to guarantee her child's happiness by making sure that failure isn't part of his vocabulary.

Before Craig can find solutions on his own, Ruby is there to show him how to do things and do them better. Jack tries to block his wife's efforts when he can. If Ruby insists on helping Craig with homework before he asks for it, Jack will say, "Why don't you let him try it on his own?"

The more energy Ruby puts into being a project coordinator and homework buddy, the less room Craig has to be himself. If Craig has an argument with a friend or is sad because he hasn't performed well on the soccer field, mom insists on doctoring his "broken heart." Ruby has even phoned other parents so that they can resolve their kids' disagreements together, instead of letting them work it out on their own. She worries constantly about Craig's well-being in the classroom and on the playground.

Ruby's lack of faith in Craig has made him a tentative person, who shies away from confrontation and bursts into tears when he is frustrated by a math problem or a challenging book. He can't stick with anything that is difficult because his mother has usurped his power. Ruby's intentions are the best, but because her behavior is motivated by unrealistic guilt, the outcome is the opposite of what she would wish.

Ruby thinks that she has stolen her son's joy by not giving him a sibling, but ironically that is not what is harming him. Guilt and overcompensation are the real culprits that prevent Craig from being himself.

Searching for Surrogate Siblings

Guilty parents of only children may succeed in raising kids who actually *do* fit the stereotypes of only children—that is, children who are clingy, withdrawn, and insecure. Parents like Ruby feel like failures and don't want their child to suffer the same fate. So they make sure that their kids always have their parachutes on, and it may be an easy ride for a while, but the landing can be rough.

Some parents spend inordinate amounts of time and energy attempting to secure a stable of playmates for their child, but what they often find is that most other families aren't as interested in this project as they are, and it hurts.

For example, Lara, a stay-at-home mom with an adopted son, Ben, can't afford to adopt again. She is weighed down with guilt, because Ben doesn't have a sibling. Lara speaks frankly about her concerns. "My husband feels that I worry too much," she says. "It seems like I am always calling and begging other people's children to come over to play, but all of the kids in our neighborhood have siblings, and they can't be with Ben all the time. As silly as it seems, I am looking for a buddy in our neighborhood who will be a constant companion for our son."

These desperate attempts to overcompensate for Ben's situation can make him feel desperate as well. If he hears his mother begging other parents to send their kids over, Ben may begin to think of himself as lonely even though he may be perfectly fine occasionally playing alone. Lara's search for a permanent buddy may not only make Ben feel different but may also prevent him from finding friends on his own. An overcompensating parent like Lara may want to fill the sibling void, but her efforts will not help her child make the most of his peer relationships.

Only children are adept at imaginative play and generally make friends quite easily. As discussed earlier, they place a high value on friendships and with little prompting from parents usually establish long and lasting relationships. Even kids with siblings don't necessarily play together all the time, so Lara's notion of a perpetual companion is a projection of her guilt.

Some parents of only children may feel guilty but are able to catch themselves before moving heaven and earth to give their child what they are certain he is missing. Little by little, Carrie Roberts and her husband, Ron, for instance, have become aware of their tendency to overcompensate.

Carrie used to bend over backward to set up play dates for their eleven-year-old, Jed. She started to obsess about keeping him busy when he was only two, because she figured the sooner the better. Carrie's solution was to borrow other people's children for an afternoon so that Jed would always have a friend around. But by the time he was eight, Jed wanted to choose his own friends or even have time to himself. "To be honest," he recalls, "sometimes she embarrassed me, because she worked so hard to make sure that I was with other kids." Jed sensed that some of those kids weren't with him because they wanted to be but because their parents had persuaded them. There were also days when he wanted to be alone to read or skateboard in the neighborhood by himself. "I know that Mom tried to make things easier for me, but I don't always want things to be easier. I just want to find my own friends and do some things my way."

"We have tried to make things easy for Jed because we feel badly that he doesn't have a brother or sister to play with," Carrie remarks. "We want everything to be wonderful for him, but we have to remind ourselves that we aren't here to remove all obstacles but to help him think things through on his own. Jed sometimes helps us with that. He'll say, 'Mom, Dad, leave me alone. I can do it myself.' We definitely tend to overparent him. But we're working on that." Now that he is older, Jed has close friendships with many different kinds of kids and gets along with almost everyone. Carrie and Ron have learned that when Jed is alone, it's not because he can't be with a friend but because he prefers it that way, at least for a while.

Carrie and Ron acknowledge that they feel guilty and have a tendency to overcompensate. They are learning to control this urge, so that they can become better parents. With Jed's assistance, they pull back, look at situations more objectively, and are allowing their son to establish friendships that are meaningful to him.

Presence, Not Presents

As we have seen with overindulgence in Chapter One, loading a child down with material possessions, extravagant parties, trips, and gifts is another way for absentee parents of only children to smooth down the sharp edges of guilt. If they had more than one child, they wouldn't spend so freely, nor would they feel as obliged to give what they know in their hearts isn't needed or sometimes even wanted.

Here's another example: Madison Richland's parents divorced when she was seven years old. Now that she is twenty-four, she looks back on her childhood both fondly and with a sense of loss. Her parents' divorce was amicable, and they shared custody of Madison. Her mother, Jessica, is a high-powered attorney and a partner in her law firm, who spent very little time with Madison while she was growing up. When she was at her mother's house, Jessica was rarely there, and Madison was cared for by a nanny, who picked her up from school and watched her until Jessica got home, usually after Madison was already asleep. Madison's mother couldn't help traveling extensively and working long hours, but she felt guilty about not being with her only child.

Madison smiles when she recalls how her mother overcompensated for her absence. Jessica made a big deal out of every holiday and birthday.

"Even St. Patrick's Day was an occasion for a lavish celebration, and we're not even Irish," remembers Madison. "I would wake up in the morning and walk down a staircase strewn with fake money, and I would follow the trail. Usually, it led to the dining room, where the table was piled with presents—all for me. On Valentine's Day, my mother designed a tree with white branches and hung presents and chocolate all over it—all for me. Christmas and Easter at her house were even more extravagant."

Madison was no different from most children and certainly enjoyed getting presents, but they didn't make her feel any better about being left alone. In fact, all of the material overindulgence made her think that something was wrong, because certainly none of her friends with siblings had Daddy Warbucks leprechauns leaving a toy store at their house.

When Madison stayed with her father, the situation was reversed. He lavished attention on her but not material possessions. "I love my mother and father, but as I look back on things, I understand that my mother's behavior was mostly motivated by guilt rather than love, and that's what bothers me the most. Of course, I would much rather have spent time with her, and I don't like thinking that my mom was that unhappy. Even now, she sends me enormous Easter and Valentine's Day care packages. So I guess she still feels pretty guilty, but it's not something I can talk about with her."

Madison had no sibling with whom to discuss this, and she couldn't say anything to her father because she didn't want to appear ungrateful, nor did she want to fuel arguments between her parents. So she accepted the gifts but not the guilt in which they were wrapped.

In families where there are two or three children, parents may have demanding jobs and have to be away from home as often as Jessica, but if they overcompensate, they have to do it for two or three, which takes a lot more money and energy. Imagine a Valentine's Day tree for three or a St. Patrick's Day celebration for four. I don't know any parents with multiple children who go to such lengths to make up for their absence and calm their guilt. Those parents rely on the fact that their kids can occupy one another, and that often suffices.

Overreacting to Normal Problems

Absentee parents may also try to overcompensate by making erratic leaps into parental realms that they usually don't visit. Parents of an only child who are immersed in their work and feel guilty about not being involved may become what I call *knee-jerk parents*. In other words, they react out of proportion to what is going on in their child's life.

For example, if they have not been paying attention to their child's academic work, and he brings home a D in math, all of a sudden these parents may decide to put on the pressure. Instead of being consistently involved and keeping track of any difficulties their child may be experiencing at school, they step in for damage control. After they have called teachers and even tutors in to "repair" things, they head back to the office, feeling better because they have played parent for the day. They were there to apply a bandage and push guilt into the background for a moment. But usually, all they accomplish is to turn the spotlight on their child, make him squirm for a while, and finally make him resentful.

No one is more acutely aware of how important he might be to his parents than an only child who is part of a close threesome. Because there are no siblings to divert his parents' attention, an only child is thoroughly tuned in to who his parents are. So if mom and dad get unduly upset over a test grade, the child of absentee parents knows that they only wear their parent hat when critical mass has been reached. He can also sense that those knee-jerk reactions stem from guilt.

Nick and Kathy, for example, are both doctors, and their son, Lyle, a ninth grader, was primarily cared for by a nanny, who had been with them since Lyle was born. Nick admits that because he and his wife work so much, they had felt extremely guilty about leaving Lyle in his nanny's care until after dinner. They relied on her to manage homework and drive Lyle to his extracurricular activities. "More often than not, we ended up being there for Lyle when things got out of hand at school or with his friends, but not on a regular basis," says Nick rather sadly. "This wasn't how we planned things, because we enjoy our son."

When Lyle's grades slipped or when he had a run-in with a teacher or another kid at school, Nick or Kathy urgently rushed in to set things straight. "Last month he came home with a C on a Spanish test," recalls Nick. "Lyle is almost fluent in Spanish, and I couldn't understand what the problem was. But instead of working with him and going over the test, I overreacted and blew up. I told Lyle that we were disappointed in *him*, when we were really more disappointed in ourselves. We felt guilty for not being the kind of parents that we should have been. His mother and I know that when we act that way, it only makes Lyle turn inward and stop communicating with us."

After Nick confronted Lyle about his Spanish grade, he got a call at his office from Lyle's school counselor, who wanted to meet with Nick and Kathy the next day. The counselor explained that the C on the Spanish test was the tip of the iceberg. All of Lyle's grades had been slipping. The former A student was quickly becoming a C and D student. In addition, teachers had been commenting that Lyle was becoming disruptive in class. The counselor explained that Nick and Kathy had to take a stronger interest in their son's daily life, because his poor grades were a cry for attention. She also told them that if they weren't careful, as Lyle got older, he might try to get attention in more self-destructive ways.

The meeting was a catalyst for a change in Nick and Kathy's life. Kathy decided to bring another doctor into her office so that she could work fewer hours. She would pick Lyle up from school and make sure that his homework was properly completed. They would try to have dinner together as a family at least three times a week and be more involved in Lyle's life overall.

Kids who have siblings aren't always as concerned about whether their parents are around or not; they like their parents' attention, but siblings provide a distraction from what might otherwise be difficult situations. Kids with siblings also have the opportunity to immediately share their frustrations and anxieties with one another, which can sometimes defuse anger. Only children will usually use their friends as a sounding board if they have trouble talking with their parents. But in serious moments, friends may not always be around, which leaves an only child no choice but to handle things as best he can on his own, at least for a short time.

Overreacting to Our Child's Demands

Probably the most painful way to receive guilt is from our own children. Often parents who feel guilty about having just one child or who are dissatisfied with the size of their family pass on that discontent to their child. Kids pick up on their parents' disappointment and become disappointed themselves. But it's good to remember that kids want to be like their friends, and if your only child's friends begin having siblings, they may start asking for one as well. In the long run, however, this doesn't necessarily mean that they really want another child to come live in their house forever. What they really want is to be like the other kids that they know.

When my daughter was four, she suddenly began asking for a sibling. I was devastated. I'm sure that she had overheard some of the conversations between my husband and me about wanting another child. No matter how carefully we tried to keep our disappointment to ourselves, it probably trickled out from phone conversations she overheard with friends, relatives, and even doctors. I'm convinced that children have hearing at least as good as bats, so I learned that if I wanted to have a private discussion about important family matters, it had to be behind closed doors or in another country.

When my daughter's best friend had a baby sister, that clinched it. She had the idea of a sibling in her head and wasn't going to let it go. I was frantic and so guilty that for some time my overcompensation was out of control. If my child wanted a sibling that badly, she must be lonely. So I made sure that she had play dates almost every day after preschool. I started her in ballet classes and thought about renting a piano so that she could begin lessons. Mozart was composing at four, and my daughter was certainly bright; perhaps she could be a budding Mozart. The piano would absorb her and stave off loneliness. Piano teachers told me that she was far too young to begin lessons, so I abandoned that plan. But during that period, it seemed that I always had my finger in a new pot of schemes to keep my daughter involved with friends or learning. She was four and five, but it wasn't enough for me to let her just be that age and enjoy it. My guilt wouldn't afford me that freedom.

If my daughter had been old enough, I probably would have helped her begin a career in law or medicine. If the child wasn't always occupied, I was sure that I had failed her. My mea culpas knew no bounds, and I became an expert breast-beater. I think that I suffered from a temporary madness, which fortunately passed by the time my daughter was six and no longer pined for a sibling. She had spent two years watching her best friend with her little sister and had decided that the sibling life was not for her. It was far too intrusive, and she liked her family the way it was. That was when I started to relax.

I don't think I did much damage in those years, primarily because my husband, bless him, was able to bring me down to earth when I got really crazy. Little did I know that I was not alone in my feelings and that there were parents of only children all over the world who felt exactly as I did and even went off the deep end temporarily.

Hannah Stone is a parent with whom I commiserate. Her biggest concern with having an only child is her son Leo's wish to have a sibling. He wants someone to play with even when they are enjoying themselves as a family at an amusement park. Hannah can't have any more children, so when Leo starts asking for a sibling, it tears her apart. She isn't sure of how to handle the intense emotions she feels, and she starts reexamining her options, which are few. Whenever Leo talks about a brother or sister, Hannah goes online and begins looking at the possibilities of adoption. She and her husband can't afford the costs, but Hannah considers borrowing money on the house or, even worse, asking her parents for a loan.

Hannah overcompensates but can't seem to stop herself. When Leo says that he wants a sibling, Hannah is on the phone immediately, arranging another play date. Sometimes they splurge at the toy store or dad will arrange a special fishing expedition.

Once, when a play date canceled, Hannah anxiously combed through the school roster looking for a child to fill in. But nothing worked out, and there was Leo looking up at her mournfully, wondering why he had to play alone. At that moment, something clicked, and Hannah realized how much emotional energy she had been expending trying to occupy Leo. She told her son that he would have to play by himself. He cried for a while, but Hannah wasn't going to appease him any longer to make herself feel better. As it turned out, once Leo got tired of the dramatics, he did quite nicely on his own.

Hannah became aware that Leo's biggest problem was not the lack of a sibling but rather parents who were always trying to make up for that lack because inside they hurt so much. Unrealistic guilt caused by circumstances beyond our control or by choices we have made that work for our family wears us down and diminishes us. No matter how we may blame ourselves, no matter what others say, no matter what our child says, at some point parents have to look at their only child and give a simple, enormous thanks for his existence. Parents should learn to respond to the guilt mongers and understand that along with passing guilt some meddlers may be rather envious of one-child families. Parents with one child have more time to give their kid, have more resources, and frequently have a closer relationship with their child than parents with more than one, who have to spread themselves thin.

What Parents Can Do About Guilt and Overcompensation

Rochelle and Marshall have jobs they love and an only child they adore. But a few years ago, they started overcompensating for having to be away from home so much. Now they have a problem with five-year-old Desiree. Rochelle has what she calls "working mother's guilt." Because she is not with Desiree during the day, she and Marshall devote all of their attention to their daughter in the evenings and on weekends. They play with her so much that Marshall has acquired an encyclopedic knowledge of Barbie's wardrobe, and Rochelle can visualize the Candyland board with her eyes closed.

But after years of amusing their daughter and acting as surrogate siblings, they are looking for a way out. "She's an active child," says Rochelle, "and doesn't go off on her own when we're home. It's gotten to the point where we feel suffocated by the demands of making her weekends and evenings fun." Although Desiree has many friends and lots of play dates, it never seems to be enough.

"She often has friends over and also has scheduled activities two nights a week," adds Rochelle, "but after her friends are out of our house for only a few minutes, she starts asking, 'What are we going to do now, Mom?' Desiree also attends an all-day kindergarten."

Overwhelmed by their situation, Rochelle and Marshall want to change the dynamics at home but know it won't be easy. They will need to start slowly. But the first thing they have to do is lock up their guilt and throw away the key.

To put change in motion, they should set aside a few minutes each day for Desiree to have alone playtime. On the first day, they can set a timer for five minutes, and then they can add five minutes each day thereafter until Desiree is playing by herself for half an hour. That is sufficient time for a five-year-old. Little by little, Desiree will learn to occupy herself without calling for mommy or daddy. If she does try to draw them into her play, they have to stand firm and refuse to join in. Once Rochelle and Marshall understand that only children can be alone without being lonely, Desiree will be a more secure child, and their family life will be more fulfilling.

If allowed enough freedom to figure things out on their own, only children become accomplished at entertaining themselves and refine this ability as they mature. It is through their alone time that they find out who they are and learn to develop their creative powers. When they get older, their ability to focus makes them better students and employees. Because they have learned how to be alone as children, they don't fear it as adults. They enjoy their own company, know themselves well, and are clear about what they want from life.

How Parents Can Avoid Overcompensation

Here are some tips to help you avoid overcompensation:

- Don't compare your family to other families. Every family is different.
- Don't blame yourself for circumstances that you can't change.
- Trust yourself. If you made the decision to have one child because it felt right to you, then it is right.
- Remember, having a sibling does not guarantee a constant companion for your child. As children get older, they can grow apart and may even dislike one another.
- When family or friends make negative comments about only children, here's what you should say: "Our family is perfect the way it is." Educate them about only children and pass what you know on to them.

Self-Test

Are You an Overcompensating Parent?

Test yourself and find out.

- Do you find yourself overscheduling your child to keep him occupied at all times?
- Do you obsess about providing your child with play dates?
- Has your child become incapable of playing by himself because you never allow him to be alone? Do you try to act as your child's sibling?
- Do you live at Toys "R" Us, waiting for the next NBA video game to arrive so that you can bring it home to your "lonely only child"?

- Do you try to make your child's life free from all pain because you feel that you have caused him enough pain already by not giving him a sibling?
- Do you find yourself overreacting when your child does something you don't like? Does your knee-jerk reaction stem from your guilt about not being there for your only one?

If you have answered yes to any of these questions, you may be a parent who overcompensates because of guilt. When we aren't preoccupied with what we think our families are missing, we raise self-assured children who take control of their lives and have compassion for others. It's our responsibility as parents to make our only children feel good about themselves, but that can't happen unless we feel good about who we are. Guilt destroys our ability to care for ourselves, and overcompensation dispirits us and makes us less than the splendid only-child families we are.

The next time someone asks why you don't have another child or suggests that your only child will grow up to be a miserable, self-centered human being, try telling him the following: "Our child is everything we ever hoped for" or "Our family is just the right size." Don't be intimidated. Don't feel guilty. Take a stand for the family you cherish.

Too many parents of only children crave what they don't have. Believing that they are missing out, they let guilt get the better of them and become so intent on justifying having one child that they strive to make him a paragon. Those parents who insist on creating the "ultimate" child commit the sin that is the subject of the next chapter: expecting perfection.

Chapter Five

Seeking Perfection

I am a seventeen-year-old only child and a senior in high school. My parents have always had very high expectations of me in everything, and I like to please them. But no matter what I do, it never seems to be enough. I studied hard for my SATs and got a combined score of 1420, which I think is pretty good. But my parents were upset because they don't think that those scores are high enough to get me into an Ivy League school. I wish that they would give me credit for the hard work I put into studying and doing my best.

Mature adults understand that there are no perfect people and no perfect lives except in our fantasies or in the movies. Yet parents of only children may still seek perfection from their child, if not all of the time, at least some of the time. Having only one child can lead to unrealistic expectations that parents with more than one don't have because all of their hopes and aspirations aren't wrapped up in one beloved, targeted package.

An only child is his parents' consummate pride and joy, their one legacy and link to immortality. Given this rarefied position in which they've placed the child, parents don't want to make mistakes, and it may be difficult for them to think of their child as anything but exceptional. When there is more than one, parents don't expect each child to do everything well, and experience teaches them that each child will have different abilities and personalities. If one child is a dreamer, who can't remember where he left his shoes, another may be a consummate list maker and organizer. One child may be enthralled by astronomy whereas the other has an extensive passion for classic cinema. Only-child parents, however, may try to raise one child to have as many good qualities as might be found in three children. One adult only child explains it this way, "It seems like you have double the bragging rights when you have two kids, but only one pool of talent with a single child. It's like having a handicap in golf."

Our society places an enormous premium on being a perfect ten. It might not be so bad if we could ignore the "tens," but they are inescapable. They assault us mercilessly from magazines, television, billboards, and buses. Their faces and the stories of their successes are almost everywhere, and before we realize it, they are a presence in our lives. The perfect ten has everything: money, fame, beauty, talent, and of course a picture-perfect family. It's enough to make parents of only children think that if they apply pressure on their child, in the right places at the right times, either overtly or covertly, their beloved child will run a Fortune 500 company by day and will be a pediatric cardiologist at night. Only-child parents give every ounce of their affection, attention, and resources to their child, so anything should be possible. With so much on the line, they may expect too great a return on their investment, which can ultimately disappoint both parents and child.

Perfectionist parents don't just *hope* that their child will reward their efforts. In subtle and not so subtle ways, they *insist*. In order to help their child achieve in school, sports, or with friends, only-child parents may unwittingly exert more pressure than their child can handle.

Yet pressure can have its positive side as well. Kids can use an encouraging push in the right direction, and it helps them find their way if they clearly understand their parents' expectations. Parents and only children have much to gain from honoring and caring for one another, so only children usually pay close attention to their parents' goals for them. That's acceptable unless and until a child begins to feel so much pressure to conform to his parents' will that he loses his individuality in the process.

How Only-Child Parents Can Apply Pressure

Pressure can be applied with a light touch or a heavy hand. It can come directly from what we say, or from how we say it, or from innuendo. It can also come from being too physically present in a child's world and watching too closely. Everything an only child does has a glow and significance that will never be duplicated. Nothing a second child does is ever as thoroughly absorbing as the first.

There are only-child parents who observe their young children as carefully as Jane Goodall watched the chimps. All these parents need is a notebook and a camera crew. They drink in everything their child does because they are thoroughly in love with her and fascinated by her behavior.

One mother of an only child recalls how she used to pass the time with her young daughter. "I was lucky to be working at home when Romy was little. I often went into her room when she was playing and watched her play for hours on end. This was when she was about three or four, and I was mesmerized by the dramas she made up with her dolls. Sometimes I could sneak in and out without her ever knowing that I had been there. At least she didn't let on that she knew because she never skipped a beat. I did this almost every day for several years."

This seems cozy, but there is a downside. Romy, now fourteen, says that she grew up feeling cherished, but she also sensed that she was always being observed. It made her secure to know that she was the center of her parents' world, but she also believes that it has made her more cautious about making decisions and more anxious to earn her parents' approval. Although Romy is close to her parents, she fears that she will let them down now that she is a teenager, because she may want to try things that will make them anxious or upset.

"My parents have always expected me to be a 'good' kid, but sometimes I just want to break out. They expect me to be perfect. You know, be a great student, do my chores, choose the right friends. It's a lot of pressure. If I had a brother or sister, I don't think they would notice me as much."

Shining a Bright Spotlight

Kids like Romy find it extremely frustrating to be the recipients of unrelenting attention. Although that attention lets them know that they are valued, it can also make them self-conscious and hesitant.

Only children are like kids on stage. When they are in the spotlight, magical things can happen, but if they make mistakes, each one stands out. It's hard for only children whose parents have been observing them intensely from birth not to feel that their every move is being weighed and judged. Fully aware of their child's strengths and weaknesses, because they are paying such careful attention, parents of an only child may be ready to offer both constructive advice and destructive criticism when their spotlight illuminates behavior or attitudes that they think require adjustment or don't fit with their values and expectations.

Only-child parents have the opportunity to be critical about and overanalyze any situation with their child. Everything the child does is front and center. For example, Grainie Corcoran comes from a large family of five but is the parent of one. She often finds herself comparing her life with her son's. In her house, Grainie was often the last child her parents noticed. It annoyed her when she couldn't get her parents' attention, but there were definitely moments when she was glad that they had so many other kids to worry about. If Grainie was practicing the piano and played poorly, there was so much noise in the house that no one could hear that she was murdering Mozart. That gave Grainie the opportunity to try new pieces without worrying that her parents would criticize her errors. It gave her a freedom that she finds difficult to give her own son.

Grainie and her husband can't seem to divert their attention from their ten-year-old only child. "Ian wanted to take up the piano last year. When he practices and plays the wrong notes, he can't just get on with it like I did because we hear everything. When he makes the same mistakes over and over, I can't stop myself from correcting him or telling him that he will never improve unless he takes more care. One part of me is trying to be helpful and encourage him, but the other part expects a lot. It's not enough for me if he is content with being mediocre because he is better than that."

Other only children can feel like specimens in a laboratory. Paige is a fifteen-year-old only child whose parents take great pleasure in pointing out her good qualities in front of friends and family, which she finds embarrassing. "I am on a club soccer team, and I guess I'm a good player, but if I make a goal or do anything out of the ordinary, my parents make a huge deal out of it. They do the same thing when I get an A on a paper. I wish they would back off, because when they tell everyone how great I am, I like it at first, but then I start to feel that I need to be that way all the time. And what if I can't be?" Paige worries that her one goal in soccer won't be enough next time, or she will always have to get A's in order for her parents to be proud of her.

Whereas Paige's parents make her squirm with their overbearing praise, sixteen-year-old Simon's parents act as if they have nothing better to do than analyze him. "When I get home from school, they ask how my day was. Sometimes I tell them it was fine when it was really lousy. But it's like they can read my mind, and they quiz me until I tell them what's bothering me. I have no privacy. If I'm really in a good mood, they want to know why, but sometimes there is no reason. They don't like it when I don't give them something to chew on." Paige and Simon both feel that there is no place to hide. Their parents are everywhere, with their magnifying glasses, looking and prying.

When parents and child are so intuitive about one another, it can be as comfortable as sinking into a favorite easy chair or as disturbing as stepping on a cactus. "Every time my parents looked at me, I thought they knew all my secrets. If I blinked differently, they noticed and asked what was going on." What was going on?

"Nothing," says Trina, a nineteen-year-old only child. "Sometimes I felt like my life was theirs." Yet Trina also enjoyed her parents' attention. "I danced and played in the orchestra when I was in high school, and they never missed a performance. I felt sorry for kids whose parents didn't show up and didn't know them as well as mine did. When I felt like it, I could talk to my parents about almost anything, which was great. But I didn't want to do that all the time, and I felt hounded when they tried to pry things out of me. It was tough to find a happy medium."

Living Vicarious Dreams

One of the most fascinating things about having a child is seeing ourselves in her, for better or worse. Even if our child is adopted and doesn't share our genes, a good part of who she is comes from what she learns from us. There is a fine line between nature and nurture. So whether you gave birth to your only child or adopted her, it's inevitable that you will hope that she will be like you in some ways and not like you in others.

Parents of only children may hope for too much, because their child means so much. They are there to make sure that he is at the top of his game or isn't repeating their mistakes. They only have one, so if that child doesn't turn out well, there are no other chances. Their success or failure as parents is intimately tied to that one child's success or failure. It can be like looking into a mirror and either seeing something pleasing or seeing something that requires plastic surgery.

Roberto is a mid-level executive with an insurance company. He has a fifteen-year-old only child, who he wishes would be more assertive. "My son, Jose, ran for president of his student council last year and lost," says Roberto forlornly. "He just wasn't aggressive enough, and it upsets me to see that, because being too ready to compromise has always held me back too. If Jose had blown his own horn more loudly, he might have won. I worry that he doesn't have enough drive. I don't want him to be like me."

Although Jose got over losing the election pretty quickly, Roberto didn't. He insisted that Jose take Tae Kwon Do to build his confidence and make him more competitive. Jose went along with the lessons but can't understand why his dad was so upset. "I didn't care that much about losing the election. My friend won, and I knew that he would do a good job, so it was OK with me. I had a good time. Dad was upset because he wanted me to win for him. But I don't care about the same things he does. Dad gets all bent out of shape over stuff that doesn't matter to me."

Then there is Rosie, a twenty-six-year-old only child who just received her master's degree in social work. Her father always wanted her to get an MBA, because he never got his and had to learn through trial and error. He dreamed that Rosie would be an accomplished businesswoman.

"I wanted to fulfill his dream because I'm the only child he has, but I just couldn't. My passion is helping people. My dad is proud of me but a little disappointed as well. Both my parents wanted me to be everything, but now they are finding out that I can only do so much."

Many parents have vicarious dreams for their children, but parents of only children may have epic visions, which often make it impossible for the child to measure up. If Baron shows an interest in science, he might get a full scholarship to MIT and discover a new galaxy. If Keisha has a talent for languages, she may become fluent in four, become a member of the diplomatic corps, and bring lasting peace to the Middle East. When parents of an only child attempt to impose their dreams on their child, life can become contentious, and no one comes out a winner.

Lani, a college sophomore, is a good example of what can happen when the dreams of an only child and her parent collide.

"My mom always wanted to be an actress but didn't have the guts to put herself out there. When I started acting in high school, and it looked like I had some talent, she went a little nuts. I think I was fourteen when she took me to get my head shots done by a professional photographer. Then she sent my photos to an agent, who took me on. It turned out that my mom was more ambitious for me than I was for myself. She pushed me to audition. When I applied to college, she wanted me to go to Juilliard, but I wanted to study journalism and creative writing, so I went to Bennington. To this day, my mom talks about what a talented actress I could have been and how I am wasting my talent. I guess I was supposed to have the career she didn't. When I look at her, I feel like I have failed, so I just don't let her get too close anymore."

The only child–parent relationship can be so tight-knit that it's a stretch for parents to separate their personal dreams from their kid's dreams. But parents who are unable to make that separation are in danger of straining or even breaking the remarkable bond they have with their child. The only child who feels like the mule for his parents' ambitions may ultimately have many achievements in life, but they will never feel like his personal achievements. He will always be working for his parents instead of being his own boss.

Competing with Other Parents

Competition is the name of the game in almost every facet of our lives. We compete for everything from jobs to parking spaces. For some of us, competition is more enjoyable than a gourmet meal, whereas others compete only because they have no choice. There is no law, however, that says we can't survive without competing through our child.

Georgia, the mother of a six-year-old only child, reluctantly confesses to having been competitive when other parents "dared" her with comments like, "My kids have always made the easiest adjustment to preschool. I never had to stay for more than two days with either of them before they were comfortable with me leaving."

"If friends said those things, I had to stand up for my one and only and prove that one could be as good as two. So my reply was, 'My daughter loves school. I sat outside her classroom for a few days, but she never even asked for me. She is so mature and independent.' I wasn't lying," Georgia adds, "just bending the truth a little, but I shouldn't have gotten sucked in at all."

Some parents of an only child think that to compete adequately with parents who have more than one, their child has to perform at a superior level in everything. It isn't enough for him to dabble in painting or fool around with a camera. There has to be seriousness of purpose and lots of it. This is true of ten-year-old Serena, who takes after-school classes at a locally renowned art center and exhibits her work. Claudio, who is fourteen, likes to cook, so his parents have enrolled him in a cooking class designed for kids who want to become chefs. A local restaurant has already named a few dishes after him. Parents of kids like Serena and Claudio feel equipped to compete with parents of more than one because their child is clearly outstanding in a specific area.

In New York City, where at least 30 percent of children are only children, the competition among parents over whose child is more advanced and "perfect" begins early. Pulitzer Prize–winning playwright Wendy Wasserstein (*Uncommon Women and Others*, 1977, and *The Heidi Chronicles*, 1988) is the parent of an only child. She found herself drawn into what she calls the Mommy Olympics. Among the parents she knew, birthday parties and play dates were occasions for urban parents to detail the considerable accomplishments of their toddlers and three- and four-year-olds. Mothers and fathers at these events spoke delightedly about how their child preferred Mozart to Mr. Rogers because they had played the *Baby Genius: Mozart* tapes when their child was an infant. When it was time to apply to preschools, the Mommy (and sometimes) Daddy Olympics gathered steam, and competition was no longer about which child slept through the night first and who had been potty trained by two, but about which child had been accepted at the most prestigious preschool.

Although Wendy Wasserstein had enough perspective to stand on the sidelines of these games and take notes, many parents of only children may not be as objective, ironic, or self-critical, so it's really hard to avoid these competitions. And for most of us, the King Kong of all competitions begins when we and our child start preparing for college admission.

If we haven't been competitive with other parents before, it soon becomes an almost unavoidable juggernaut. Before we know it, we are gathered at school events, sharing information about GPAs, SATs, extracurricular accomplishments, athletic or musical prowess, teacher recommendations, internships, and the momentous college essay. We want to know where our child stands in comparison with everyone else, to give us a sense of what he is facing and what we can do to make him more competitive.

"Rebecca scored a 1500 on her SATs. She did much better than her older sister, who got into Penn, so she may make it to Yale." The parent of an only child might hear this and swallow hard. "Wow, they are probably going to have two kids in Ivy League schools. I hope that my one can do that well."

The temptation to compare an only child with other parents' kids can be overwhelming. Parents with more than one have a longer brag sheet than parents with one, and the competitive only-child parent may not be able to stand the thought that his child might not have as many talents and accomplishments as two. So when Jack begins bragging that colleges are already scouting his daughter, who plays club soccer, and that his son got into Harvard, the parent of an only child may flaunt her child's skills as captain of the basketball team and editor of the school newspaper. If this chatter could be kept among parents, it might not be so bad, but kids always find out what we say about them. Parental rivalry adds to the tremendous tension that most kids already feel when they start thinking seriously about college.

Only-child Johnna Siegel has been playing softball for three years and is a gifted pitcher. She started playing for the love of the game, but now that she is in tenth grade, her parents are insisting that she think about using her abilities to attract the interest of college scouts. They have hired a private coach and barring any serious injuries think that she could get a full athletic scholarship at a prestigious school.

"I want my daughter to be somebody," her mother says. "I never finished college and always regretted it. We can't afford to finance her education like most of her friends' parents, so she needs to find a way to do it playing ball." It wouldn't be enough for Johnna's parents if she were to attend a local two-year college and later transfer to a state university. "I couldn't stand going to graduation and listening to other parents talk about all the great colleges their kids are planning to attend," adds Johnna's mother. "We have only one special child, and we want her to live up to her potential." But they have to be careful, because Johnna may either crack under the pressure or decide to give up playing because it's no longer fun. If they were to encourage Johnna's love of the game and let her choose how to use her talents, she would be more likely to fulfill her promise.

Being Overly Critical

Perfectionist parents are frequently critical parents. It goes with the territory. If you expect everything to be "just so," you will have to make it that way. In order to do that, you will ask your only child to do things your way: "the right way." Parents can express their disapproval verbally or through nonverbal communication, which includes body language and facial expressions. Some only children are so good at reading their parents that they can sense what their parents are thinking without hearing a word or seeing an eye twitch.

Larry, a twenty-five-year-old only child, says that his parents never even had to tell him that they were unhappy with something he had done. "We are so close that I know all of my parents' mannerisms. It sounds weird, but I can tell that they are angry when they breathe a certain way."

Some parents take the direct route to criticism and start when their child is young. They may expect a great deal from their only child because they think of him as so capable and gifted, even though he is probably just a normal kid experiencing the usual developmental milestones. These parents often criticize in an effort to "improve" their child and motivate him.

Parents who compare their only child with other children overtly or covertly are often being critical but may not see it that way. They think that if they give their child a lofty example to follow, it will spur him on to greater heights.

Taylor Bachrach's mother had infinite suggestions about how Taylor could advance herself. She also frequently compared Taylor with other kids. Although her mother meant no harm, it generated a lot of guilt and resentment. "My mother used to think that I could do anything. After all, I'm her only one and a genius in her eyes," says Taylor.

"My mom's favorite phrase was, 'You could do that.' When my friend Shelly decided to apply to medical school, my mother pointed out that I could do that too, even though I had only taken one science course in college and my major was comparative literature. All I would have to do is go back to school for two years to take my science classes, get fabulous scores on the MCAT, and do a summer internship in a clinic in Africa. I have another friend who is an investment banker and makes lots of money. My mother told me that I could do that too. All I would have to do is—well, you can guess the rest."

Taylor's mother never considered herself to be judgmental. Instead she felt that she was complimenting her daughter by telling her that she could do almost anything because she was so exceptional. When Taylor explained that those kinds of comparisons made her feel ashamed about deciding to be a teacher, her mother was shocked that her words, meant to be encouraging, had been taken as criticism.

Critical parents are nitpickers, and no one can pick nits as well as parents of only children, because they are so focused on their one child. There is always something that can be improved.

"I like to read *Goosebumps* books," nine-year-old Logan says, "but when my mom sees me reading them, she gets angry and calls it trash. She wants me to read stuff like *Harry Potter*." So Logan has put *Goosebumps* away and has started *Harry Potter*, which is not as much fun for him.

Fourteen-year-old India has grown up in a household where routines and rules are well established, and her parents expect things to be done a certain way.

"When I clean my room, it has to be done the way my mother wants it. If she comes in and sees that I've made my bed but have some piles of clothing, books, or papers around, she will point and ask what they are doing there. She will say, 'Do you want to put these things away?' But I don't want to put them away. I have my own system and ideas about where things should go. But when I clean up my way, my mother thinks that I have small animals living under my bed. She stands there and makes sure that the piles disappear. Then I can't find anything."

When parents are always watching and judging, only children may feel angry, but because their parents are so important to them, they will still try to please their parents before they please themselves. This makes it difficult for only children to relax and find their own level of competence.

If you have only one child, why can't she be everything? This includes being good-looking, popular, well mannered, intelligent, respectful, and successful at everything she undertakes—all at the same time. In short, why can't she be perfect?

Why can't they all be like America's national security advisor, and only child, Condoleezza Rice? She was raised by parents who demanded extraordinary things from her, and they got them. There was nothing that Rice wouldn't be capable of accomplishing. She played the piano and became a concert pianist. She entered college when she was fifteen, had white-glove manners, and was always perfectly groomed. She speaks a number of languages and began teaching at Stanford when she was twenty-seven. She believed that she could do anything, a notion encouraged by her parents and one that she has applied to every endeavor.

Condoleezza Rice's parents might not have asked for so much from one person if they had had more than one child. But Condoleezza was expected to fulfill all of their dreams with poise and unerring ambition.

For some parents, the quest for perfection is more superficial. Eleven-year-old Lila has a style all her own, but it's one that annoys her parents. A tomboy, who chooses to wear overalls and baggy pants, she prefers to shop at Goodwill. Her friends are "girly" girls, who follow the latest teeny-bop trends. Instead of admiring their daughter's individualism, Lila's parents are always picking at her about her dress and comparing her with other kids. "My parents think I'm sloppy," remarks Lila, "but I'm happy this way. Mom and Dad want me to be somebody else. Maybe if I had a sister who dressed the way they think I should, they would get off my back."

Because only children don't have the company of brothers and sisters, their parents live in fear that their child will be unpopular outsiders. This can drive them to be critical of how their child spends his free time.

Seven-year-old Owen started reading well when he was six. An exceptionally bright child, he still enjoys dramatic play with his trucks and Legos and has become an avid reader. He likes nothing better than to curl up with a book or hang out in his room for a few hours on the weekend. Although his parents are thrilled with Owen's intelligence and support his interests in science, math, and reading, they want the "whole package." He should not only be intellectual but extremely social as well. They worry constantly that he doesn't spend enough time with friends, and they tend to make play dates for Owen that he doesn't necessarily want. Although Owen appears to be content, his parents keep pressing him to be more social. Owen's parents act as if their son is not "enough."

Consequences of Perfectionism

The idea that we can design our only child to embody our hopes for her, and in some cases for ourselves, has long-ranging consequences. Some of the effects of searching for perfection can be positive, but many are negative.

Negative Consequences

Encouraging our only children to be and do everything creates confusion, because it can inhibit decision making, resulting in a child who is overwhelmed by choices.

If a child thinks that he can (or should) "do it all," he may not understand how to make the sacrifices necessary to do a few things well. The only child who realizes that he may not be able to pursue all of his dreams at the same time can become frustrated and unhappy. Ambitious only children can be very hard on themselves, especially when they expect to do as well as the adults they revere. This can lead to insecurities when the child realizes that his performance doesn't live up to his ideals.

Twenty-one-year-old Sawyer, for example, is an only child who has just graduated from college. He is back living at home with his parents while he decides what to do next. His biggest problem is making choices, because he wants to pursue several of his interests. When he was a child, he was involved in activities ranging from basketball to local theater groups. He thinks that he can be successful in many areas, because his parents encouraged his interests and made him believe that he could do it all. Now he has no idea what direction he wants to follow. "I wake up every morning thinking about how I can be more successful. I look at other people and think that I should be doing what they are doing. I'm never satisfied with myself and am convinced that I should always be doing more. I'm really anxious and paralyzed by indecision."

Only children who are pursued by demons pressing them to do more and do better may be the ones who don't want to experiment because they are afraid they won't succeed and will look like failures in their parents' eyes.

"I was really excited about taking an advanced placement biology class this semester," says sixteen-year-old Beatrice. "But then I started thinking about how my parents would feel if I didn't get an A in the class. I've always gotten A's. So I decided to take a regular bio class instead. My parents have done everything for me, and I would hate to let them down." Beatrice feels so responsible for her parents' happiness that she has put hers on the back burner. Unless Beatrice's parents make it clear that she needs to satisfy herself as well as them, she will never be able to get the best out of her adolescent years.

Both parents and child should recognize that being too obligated to one another can be treacherous. Parents must assure their only child that although they want her to do well, they don't always expect her to be a star. In fact, they hope that she will make the kinds of decisions that will lead her to rethink who she is and what she values as she matures. The only child should reassure her parents that she will try to make them proud but not at the expense of self-discovery.

An only child who feels deeply indebted to his parents may try to be everything they hope for him. He may strive to be as popular as his father or as academic as his mother.

"I was the social chairman of my fraternity," remarks Dean. "Believe me, it helped a lot in business later on. I hope that my son is as outgoing as I was." Actually, Dean's only son, Norm, tends to be quite a bit more reserved than his dad. But when he was a sophomore in high school, he decided to make a change and become part of the popular group, because he knew it would make his dad happy. That group of kids spent their free time partying and using drugs and alcohol. Norm felt uncomfortable with this behavior but joined in so that he would be liked. His social life soared, and his father was happy to hear Dean's phone ring several times a day. For a while, Norm continued to do well in school and hung out with his new friends on weekends. Ultimately, however, his partying got out of control, and his grades began to suffer. Once his parents found out what was going on, Dean felt responsible and realized he had forced his son into making poor choices just to please him.

Only children who are preoccupied with being perfect may lose the ability to empathize with others, because they are so intent on achieving their goals.

This is what happened to Deirdre. Her parents were unrelenting in their desire for her to be the best, so everything she did in high school and college was calculated to advance the career she wanted in law. She graduated from college Phi Beta Kappa and was admitted to one of the best law schools in the country. She had arrived at her destination but in the process had neglected her friends and ignored her boyfriend. When she graduated from law school, her parents wanted to throw her a party, but Deirdre realized that she had very few friends to invite. She had broken up with her boyfriend because she didn't have the time for him, and a number of her friends had stopped calling. Even when a friend's parent passed away, Deirdre found it difficult to offer much support because she was so distracted by the demands of exams and papers. Deirdre needed to get where she was going and had to get there "now," but she failed to remember why she was there at all.

Parents of only children who insist that their child pursue a discipline they favor may get the desired response. But this can backfire when the child becomes an adult and finds out that he is not suited to the profession.

For example, Boris, a forty-three-year-old heart specialist, is the only child of two doctors. From the time he was a little boy, it was "understood that I would go into 'the family business.'" Boris's parents are Russian immigrants, who worked extremely hard to create a successful life for themselves in America. Because Boris was the only child, there was even greater pressure for him to become a doctor.

"If I had siblings, the expectation wouldn't have been as intense. Certainly, they may have expected one of us to become a doctor, but it would have been much easier to forge my own way in life." Science came easily to Boris, and his years in medical school went smoothly. "I never really stopped to think about whether or not this was really what I wanted to do. I never felt free to explore any other options because as the only child, I felt so compelled to gratify my parents." Unfortunately, Boris's years as a doctor have proven to be unsatisfying. In midlife, he finds himself wondering what else he might do. With a family to support, this is obviously not the ideal time for Boris to "go searching," but because he was never given this opportunity when he was younger, he feels that he can't be happy until he makes a change.

Boris's situation raises some common questions faced by many only children: "How am I different from my parents?" and "If I don't do what they want the way they want it done, will they still love me?" An only child who is buried under expectations and believes that parental love is conditional may too willingly surrender to his parents' desires. As in Boris's case, this may result in detachment from one's true self.

Only children who consistently strive for perfection may think that nobody can do anything as well as they can.

Ostensibly, this would seem like a sign of strength and confidence. But people like that have difficulty delegating responsibility and overload themselves with a to-do list longer than Martha Stewart's party strategies.

"Something as simple as a dinner party," says Cabbane, an only child and attorney, "is enough to turn me into Stalin. Sure, I'll tell someone to bring a salad and another person to bring wine, but there's no way I'd actually let them bring the salad they wanted to make or the wine that they love. I'm so afraid that someone will bring something atrocious that I'll tell them exactly what to buy. This drives my husband and my friends crazy. Most of the time, whether it's a potluck at home or a business meeting, I'll plan each detail and micromanage everyone involved. I can barely give my assistant a decent workload when I know I could just do it all on my own and have things done exactly as I want. Ironically, this makes me resentful that I'm doing all of the work, even though I've taken it on myself."

Positive Consequences

Believe it or not, there are positive consequences to the search for perfection. Granted, they are fewer than the negative consequences, but they are powerful nonetheless.

When only children know that their parents have high expectations of them, they can be intensely motivated to achieve. Kids whose parents expect little of them have little to give. Only children expect to perform well and usually want to reward their parents' devotion.

"If I weren't an only child, I probably would not be where I am today," says twenty-seven-year-old investment banker Brad Rogers. "I think that I'm basically lazy and would have taken the easy way out of most things if my parents had not been right there all the time. They made sure that I did my homework, took the appropriate classes, and worked hard. When I was disorganized, they helped me get things together. I wasn't allowed to let things go. Now I have a system that I use to stay organized. I have a lot of self-discipline, and since I run my own business, that's important."

A child who does things well will be more confident about himself.

Only children who strive and achieve their goals understand what success means. "My parents told me that I could have anything I wanted if I went about it the right way," says only child Chandra Setti. "Most of my friends' parents would have said, 'Dream on.' Now I am the one forcing my friends to try bigger and better things. They have no one in their lives to ask the best of them the way I did. My friends complain, 'This is going to be so hard or impossible,' and I tell them that it is possible if they want it badly enough. I was expected to 'go for the gold,' so I guess I think they should too. I felt comfortable taking risks because I had my parents as support, and we were so close. I want to be there for my friends that way too."

When parents don't allow their child to do things halfway and insist that he stay motivated, that training is often an important factor in an only child's success.

Marcus Thomas is an only child whose parents made him stay with a choice even when it didn't look as if it would work. Marcus took up soccer when he was seven. It was challenging for him, and two weeks into the new season he begged his parents to let him quit. His parents refused. "I thought you wanted to make goalie this year. We won't let you quit until you do that. Then at the end of the season, we will see if you still hate it," his mother responded firmly. Marcus ended up becoming goalie, and his team won the championship. "I'm really glad that my mom didn't let me quit," he says. Marcus learned firsthand that even when things seem very difficult, he can prevail.

How Parents Can Avoid Destructive Perfectionism

We have seen that perfectionism has both positive and negative aspects. But in order to maintain perspective so that we don't burn out our only child, there are a few things to keep in mind:

- Put your lab tools away. Your child is not a specimen.
- Stop examining and analyzing every facet of his behavior.
- Put some emotional distance between you and your child. Remember that you are different people with very distinct needs and desires.
- Separate love from approval. One does not depend on the other. According to Carl Pickhardt, "Love is unconditional but approval must be earned."[1]
- Work on knowing who your child really is as opposed to who you want him to be.
- Support your child's differences. Don't compare your child with others. Each person is unique.
- Accept the fact that your child will sometimes make poor decisions and that he will learn from them. Perfection is for God not humans.

Self-Test

Are You a Perfectionistic Parent?

Test yourself and find out.

- Do you find yourself becoming frustrated because you feel that your child isn't as advanced as other children his age?
- Do you criticize and correct your child's work even when he is still learning to do something new?
- Do you expect your child to do everything well and be a winner at all times?
- Do you find yourself insisting that your child take part in activities in which he has little or no interest?
- Does your child complain that nothing he ever does is good enough to satisfy you?
- Is your child tense and afraid to take risks because he is afraid that he might fail?

If you answered yes to any of these questions, you may be a perfectionistic parent. Perfectionistic parents of only children may be misled into thinking that their only child can or should be far above average because he seems so mature. But that mature appearance is the result of spending a great deal of time around adults and absorbing their mannerisms and customs. Your child is still a child, not a grown-up. The next chapter discusses the sin of treating an only child as if he were one of us.

Chapter Six

Treating Your Child like an Adult

I am a sixteen-year-old only child with great parents. But being an only child isn't much fun because my house is always so quiet and everything has to be kept so neat. I'm jealous of my friends and cousins who have siblings, and there's always something going on in their houses: music, computer games, food fights, shooting hoops out back. I even like it when the kids dis and tease each other. It's also fun because when I am there, I don't have to be grown-up. At my house, my parents are always talking about books, their work, their adult friends, politics, more work—and they expect me to join in. Most of the time, I feel like I can't be a real kid when I'm at home with my parents. Help!!

Only-child parents may think of their family as the Three Musketeers: they eat together, travel together, and socialize together, even when the events they attend are mainly for adults. With two adults and only one kid, it's inevitable that the majority rules, the child is outnumbered two to one, and the focus is more on adult concerns and activities. In families with more than one child, there's an entirely different dynamic, one in which the odds are even or may even be in favor of the kids. Those parents with more than one child are also less inclined to include their children in adult-oriented events, such as dinner parties and art openings. Controlling two or three bored kids at an elegant cocktail party is a task we might only wish on our enemies, but supervising one doesn't take a posse.

Parents with only one child may be reluctant to hire a babysitter when they want to go out because it's so easy to bring seven-year-old Elijah along. After all, he has good manners and knows the kind of behavior that is acceptable in adult settings. But even though an abundance of togetherness is one of the things that makes having an only child so enjoyable, it can also be a source of anxiety for a child who associates pleasing his parents with behaving like an adult. In his heart, Elijah might rather be hanging out with his friends, playing video games, or kicking a soccer ball. He may think that his parents only care about his life when he is "part of the team," but not about his life as a kid. This may make him feel isolated and jealous of friends with siblings, whose lives may seem more interesting and playful.

Creating a home that is child centered when there is just one child takes a bit of effort, whereas with two or three children, the adults never outnumber the kids. For a child who thinks that adults are always in charge of the game plan, life may begin to feel like a succession of boring obligations. Only-child parents, who have included their child in so much of their adult life, may expect their kid to have a sophistication and worldliness more suited to the parents' own peer group. The child feels compelled to act the part of hostess at a dinner party, learn to speak quite knowledgeably about an aspect of her parents' business, or feel obliged to take on responsibilities for which she is not yet emotionally equipped. Although some exposure to culture and worldly issues may be interesting to an only child, young children are not really that interested in our business problems, political views, or the menu at a new, well-reviewed restaurant. It can become so pleasurable for parents of an only child to have a miniature adult by their side that they may lose sight of the fact that their kid needs to be a kid. The child who becomes a sophisticated sidekick has crossed over into a world in which she can never truly fit. Her parents, however, may feel that it's a perfect fit for them and may even try to limit her interaction with other children in an attempt to keep her to themselves.

Only children can be "adultified" in other ways as well. They may be given too strong a voice in family decisions, which empowers them to think that they can do what adults do even though they lack adult reasoning skills and life experiences. A child who is given this kind of power may even think that he's part of his parents' marriage and that he has a say in how conflicts are resolved. This may lead him to feel responsible when there's a divorce, and in a more serious case, an illness or death. This child may find himself completely overwhelmed when he is faced with the task of helping to care for one or both parents. In the case of the single parent, the only child may be too involved in a parent's dating and may take on the role of confidante and even surrogate significant other.

Yet there is a bright side to this. Only children who spend substantial time with adults are likely to be more relaxed when they have to deal with teachers, job interviews, and meeting new grown-ups. They frequently have a self-assurance and comfort in the world beyond home that is unusual for kids with siblings. But it is possible for an only child to have this same competency without relinquishing his childhood or sense of place. It's up to parents to set proper divisions between child and adults. Parents should provide the right conditions for their only child to fully enjoy childhood under the shelter and in the company of adults he both loves and admires.

How Parents Can Prevent Childhood

Only children should never feel that they must sprint through childhood to get to adulthood. Childhood is a process to be savored, not a race to a finish line. Every only child should be guaranteed the right to take that journey at his own pace and in his own fashion. Parents who lose sight of this deprive their child of the emotional strength he will need to become a secure adult.

Daily interaction with only children can be intense for everyone. If we are having a bad day or feeling sad, it's hard to keep it from our child. If we are struggling with a decision, such as changing jobs, moving, or dealing with a sick parent, we may discuss these things in private, but our preoccupation can make us distracted, and a young child may notice. She may begin asking questions about why we are behaving differently, and we may feel the need to provide answers.

In searching for those answers and in a desire to maintain the close communication we have come to expect from our child, we may give her more information than she can handle or may ask her to help make decisions that only an adult should make. Parents need to make a clear separation between their adult lives and their child's life.

There are times when sharing is important, times when it's necessary to be quiet, and times to dole out information in small pieces that can be easily digested. As a child grows and is able to handle more details about adult issues, we can explain more.

Including a Child Too Much

It's not unusual for only children to be included in parental discussions about important matters that may affect the family, because there are only three people interacting with one another. Conversations at the dinner table may be about how much it will cost to buy a new car, whether or not they can afford a vacation, or what's the best way to handle conflicts at work. Many parents think that they should tell their only child almost everything, because they don't want to be like their parents, who kept them in the dark. They don't want their child to find out that they've been hiding things or keeping secrets. What these parents forget, however, is that there are many private and disturbing things about life that children are simply too young to understand, and they don't need or want all of that information. In fact, it confuses and frightens them.

Without the maturity to fully understand that conflicts among grown-ups at work can be resolved and that what we can't afford today, we may be able to afford tomorrow, the only child may become an inveterate worrier, who thinks he needs to find solutions to adult problems. Here's a case in point: ten-year-old Cal began to notice that his mother, Astrid, was increasingly moody. She began to pick on him for little things, and he began asking if anything was wrong. At first, Astrid said no, but one day when they were out shopping, Cal asked if he could have a pair of the latest and hottest athletic shoes. Usually, Astrid would have said, "Not now. Maybe later." But family finances were strained, and Astrid had just found out that she might lose her job in a flurry of companywide layoffs. There was no way that they could live on her husband's salary alone, and she was resentful. So this time, she let it all out and launched into a tirade about Cal's father and their financial situation. "You know, Cal, this isn't a good time. I may lose my job tomorrow, and your father doesn't seem to care about making more money. He's lazy and doesn't want to push himself. If he would try a little harder, maybe we wouldn't be in this situation."

Cal asked if they would have to move and if they could still go to movies and whether he would have to give up his karate lessons. A whole universe of worries assaulted him. An only child like Cal, who is made privy to adult problems, wants to try to solve them. He may think that he has that ability because his parents have solicited his opinion about so many things.

Parents who reveal too much about their health issues can be asking an only child to grow up far too quickly. Raul is a thirty-five-year-old only child and artist, who has felt guilty and responsible for his parents ever since he can remember. "I don't know if I was ever really a kid," he says. "My parents included me in everything, and I mean everything. I knew more about my mother's uterus than I ever wanted to know. They never bothered to keep much behind closed doors because they made me a party to everything else." Here's what happened:

When he was about seven, Raul began asking his parents if he would ever have a brother or sister. His mother told him that they had been trying but that she had had a few miscarriages and had given up on having more children. She also told Raul, with a tinge of bitterness, that his father never really wanted another child, and she had to convince him to keep trying. If they had started thinking about it sooner, maybe she wouldn't have miscarried so many times.

Although Raul had been taught the basics of baby making, he had no idea that babies could be there one minute and gone the next. He was shocked and thought about this phenomenon for some time. But no matter how much he pondered the loss of a baby, he couldn't shake the idea that somehow he was to blame for his mother's problem. Perhaps if he had been a better son, his father would have wanted another child sooner. Then he would have had a brother (his ideal), and everyone would be happy.

From the time his mother told him about the miscarriages, Raul worried that something terrible might happen to her and that she could also disappear, like the unborn babies. In seeking out Raul's sympathy, his mother had set him adrift. If she had simply told Raul that it would be lovely to have another child someday, but they were perfectly happy with him, Raul would have felt comforted and safe. She could have waited until Raul was much older to give him information about miscarriages. Too much information means having to juggle too many new fears.

Forgetting There's a Child in the House

Only children can often sound so sophisticated and deep that they frequently seem older than their years. Their vocabularies and mannerisms may be more advanced than those of other children their age, but parents should not be tricked into thinking that their only child is some kind of prodigy.

In reality, these kids have only their parents to model themselves after, so copying adult language and behaviors comes naturally. They are able to create the illusion of maturity, but they are still kids.

One twelve-year-old only child loves it when adults tell her that she seems so much older than her age. "I think it's cool that so many grown-ups think I'm sixteen. I guess I have a good vocabulary, and I like talking to my parents' friends." Parents can find their child's apparent maturity dazzling, but it's a fool's gold that can lead to unrealistic expectations on all sides.

In a household where parents assume that their child is one of them, everything will be organized to suit adult tastes. "My house is perfect," says ten-year-old Rhonda, with a mixture of pride and regret. "All of the furniture in the living room is white and my room is really pretty. I like having my friends over, but most of the house is off-limits to us. I'm always afraid that someone will get something dirty. So I usually play at my friends' houses."

Rhonda's parents like to cook gourmet food and hate clutter. They believe that their daughter's taste is similar to theirs and that she enjoys a life free of disorder. Rhonda would hate to hurt her parents' feelings, so she doesn't tell them that what she enjoys most about playing at friends' houses where there are siblings is precisely the noise and clutter she finds there. When she gets home, it takes her awhile to get used to how quiet and clean everything is. She loves her parents but feels that being a kid is an intrusion on their way of life.

Some only children are not only expected to live in spotless homes and keep them that way but are also expected to be miniature adult hosts and hostesses when their parents' friends come to visit or have dinner.

"It's always been my job," says thirteen-year-old Barry, "to serve hors d'oeuvres, take coats, and chat with guests. I kind of entertain them until my parents come downstairs. I think it started when I was about five. When I was little, I thought it was kind of fun, but now I feel like a robot. I talk differently around grown-ups than I do around my friends. It's weird, and I don't like to be the host as often as my parents want me to."

Although Barry has developed excellent manners and usually likes his parents' friends, he would much rather be instant messaging his own friends or watching a favorite TV show on a Saturday night. Even the most well-brought-up only child will feel like an extraterrestrial if he has to spend too much time with his feet firmly planted in the adult world.

Overexposure to the Good Life

An only child tends to be portable, whereas two or three are more difficult to transport, especially if parents have their sights set on trips to foreign countries. Even with travel bargains, it's still more expensive to buy four airplane tickets than three. One of the great luxuries of having an only child is being able to take her with you and share life with her. Travel to other countries gives children a perspective that a day at a mall or a weekend in Las Vegas can't provide.

Twelve-year-old only child Eli has spent every summer since he was a baby in Europe with his parents. He has also been to Australia, Bali, Fiji, and Japan. As a result, he loves to travel, but there were many vacations when he would have gladly traded his luxury hut in Fiji or the chic hotel near the Champs-Elysées for the beach at home, where he could have been playing volleyball with his friends.

"Sometimes I can bring a friend with me," says Eli thoughtfully, "but usually it's just me and my parents. I get bored being with them, but at least I have my Game Boy." Eli appreciates what he has learned from traveling, but if he were offered a choice, he would rather stay at home and skateboard with the neighborhood kids.

Another way that only-child parents with the best of intentions adultify their kids is by dragging them along to cultural events, such as opera and ballet. These children's lives are certainly enriched by their exposure to music and art, but parents who mandate long afternoons in museums listening to docents discuss the influence of Spanish artists on French painting or three hours of Brahms are overdoing it and are expecting their young children to have too many adult tastes and for too long a stretch.

"My husband and I chose to have an only child, so we could go places and do things together easily," says China.

"We were excited when our daughter, Jenny, showed an interest in art and started taking her to museums when she was about five. But we didn't go to the Sunday afternoon kids' events. No, we wanted her to know what it was like to look thoroughly at a painting. I have a pretty good background in art, so I gave her clues about what to look for. If we went to an exhibit, we stayed until we saw everything. Usually, Jenny wanted to go home after fifteen minutes, but we refused to leave even though she got so bored, she was more interested in playing with her hair than looking at art. But now that Jenny is fourteen, she refuses to go with us and won't even step inside a museum unless it's for a school trip, when she doesn't have a choice."

Only-child parents are quick to think that if their bright child shows an interest in art, music, ballet, or basket weaving, it's necessary to call in the big guns. They find their child the best piano teacher in the city or spend hours in museums. It's not enough for their child to have interests and explore them in a casual way. Instead those interests are often channeled and pursued in a directed, adult manner. Jenny liked to paint and enjoyed looking at Van Gogh, but at age five she wasn't ready to become an art historian.

Only children who have the opportunities that Jenny and Eli have are lucky to have an education that is enhanced. Their life as children, however, may not be ideal. Parents of only children must curb their enthusiasm for trying to make their child older than she is. I know that the temptation is enormous, but in order to avoid the sin, remind yourself of your child's chronological age, and try not to be flattered when other adults say, "Oh, Jerzey is only ten? He seems so much older." It's not necessarily a compliment.

Making Your Child a Part of Your Marriage

In earlier chapters, I have talked about the necessity of boundaries to keep your only child from becoming one of those "hideously spoiled" only children that we hear about so often. One of the most dangerous areas where poor boundaries can be very destructive is in your marriage.

An only child usually has a strong voice in the family, so it's not surprising for her to think that she is an integral part of her parents' relationship. Two parents and an only child form a triangle—with the only child at the top. If she is allowed to takes sides in quarrels between parents or thinks that she should be the one to settle things, she is taking on an adult role not appropriate for her age or position in the family. If she aligns herself with one parent against another, the structure becomes unbalanced. Marriage should be the province of parents, but that is easier to see in theory than it is in practice when an only child is involved.

Because 50 percent of marriages end in divorce, it's likely that your only child will have friends with divorced parents. Even very young children understand that divorce is painful and that it causes serious disruptions. When parents in an only-child household argue, their child may begin to fear that the disagreement, however minor, will end in divorce. That's what my child thought, and other only children agree that they have had similar fears.

Only children are often sensitive to their parents' relationship in a way that kids with siblings are not. In a family with siblings, if parents argue or disagree, there is a chance that the kids won't hear it or won't give it as much weight, because they are occupied with one another and aren't part of a triangle. In sibling families, the kids may unite to get what they want from parents, but it is less common for them to pit one parent against another or to get in the middle of a parental quarrel.

Here's an example: Thalia is an eighteen-year-old only child who just left home for college. She and her parents were always so close that she thought their marriage absolutely included her. "We did so much together that it was natural for me to think that I was part of their marriage. I used to get upset when they wanted to go away without me. I couldn't understand why they wouldn't want me with them, and I gave them a very hard time about it. I tried to make them feel guilty, so they wouldn't leave me, and sometimes it worked. If they had to attend an event where children weren't welcome, I wanted to know exactly why I couldn't go, and I would argue with them." Thalia still has a difficult time thinking about her parents without her. "We are a threesome," she says definitively. Some only children don't just complain about not being a member of the team, they also try to have a say in decisions that parents should be making with each other.

Twenty-seven-year-old Jasper remembers when his parents were trying to decide which car to buy. "I think it was between a Volvo and a Honda. They were sitting at the kitchen table with the brochures spread out in front of them when I walked in. I must have been eleven or twelve. I looked at the brochures and said, I like the Honda. I vote for that one. My mother told me that I could have an opinion, but I didn't have a vote, and it was their decision. She told me that buying a car was a big expense and since I didn't drive yet, it was something that had to be decided between her and my dad. I got really mad and told them that I wouldn't ride in the car unless they bought the one I liked. I was so used to having a say in household decisions, like what color to paint the living room or what to have for dinner, that I didn't want to give up that control."

Once parents give a kid the idea that he can be part of big decisions, he will expect to be involved in elements of a marriage that are inappropriate for him. "For the past year, my husband has not been home much," says Nadine. "His work has taken him out of town, or he has been at the office fourteen hours a day. I hardly ever see him. We got into a big fight over it, and our son, Monty, who is twelve, heard us and defended me. It wasn't right for him to get in the middle, but since he has no brothers or sisters, he is very involved in our lives and feels like he is responsible in some way for our happiness. I was secretly grateful to him for saying something because it helped my argument. But I know that it upset him."

Unless Nadine provides a separation between Monty and her marriage, her son will continue to want to take sides, which can only make difficult situations worse. In addition, Monty will worry needlessly about his parents' relationship. Nadine should have told Monty that she and his father would work things out together in their own way.

Role Reversals

When a parent or parents are ill, an only child may become an essential caregiver. Darcy has been caring for both her parents for as long as she can remember. Her mother has had three hip replacements, and her father suffers from a heart condition. When she was trying to decide which college to attend, her decision was largely influenced by her parents' health. She had always been there for them, so she decided not to go out of state for school and to stay as close to home as possible.

"I felt guilty leaving at all," says Darcy. "They do have strong interests of their own, so I didn't worry so much about the empty-nest syndrome, but my mom depended on me to be there to listen to her worries and concerns." Darcy's mother depended on her emotionally so much that in effect their roles were reversed. Darcy became the parent and her mother, the child. Instead of creating her own support system with their large extended family and friends, Darcy's mother leaned almost totally on her daughter. She felt that only Darcy could really understand what was happening in their family.

Having taken the role of parent for so long, Darcy now notices a pattern in her friendships and relationships. She is always trying to fix things for people and needs to be in command. If she isn't mothering someone, she doesn't feel fulfilled. She has lost sight of herself and now realizes that she hardly ever takes her own wants and needs into consideration.

When Parents Are Divorced

Only children of divorced parents can also become caregivers for themselves, at least part of the time. No matter how well intentioned, parents who share custody may find themselves letting their child take responsibility for organizing a life that moves back and forth from one house to another. Because so many only children seem older than their years, parents may think that they are capable of strategizing and prioritizing the way adults do.

"My parents divorced when I was eleven. They are still friends, but they both work a lot. I spend half the week at my dad's and half the week at my mom's," says fifteen-year-old Grant. "It was hard enough to get used to them living apart, but then I had to remember to bring stuff with me and not forget my homework. At first, my parents would leave a list of things for me to pack, but after a year or so they got too busy, and I had to do it myself. I forgot a lot of things, but after I left my basketball uniform at my dad's and couldn't play, I was better about keeping track of things."

Then there is the only child who has to adjust to separate rules and parenting styles in two households. If parents don't have a system for communicating with each other and a shared philosophy about how to raise children, it gives an only child an opening to direct her own life. Be careful!! Only children enjoy taking over and will do it if you give them an inch.

"My parents divorced when I was seven, because they could hardly agree about anything—and they still can't," recalls twenty-two-year-old Neil. "But they did decide to share custody of me."

Neil's father checked his homework, specified curfews, and insisted on manners. His mother, however, indulged Neil's whims. She made him special food, let him watch TV during the week, and "assumed" that he would get his schoolwork done. "Actually, I was a pretty responsible kid," he continues, "and most of the time I did what I was supposed to do, but I definitely had fun playing both ends against the middle. If my mom said that I could do something that my father would never let me do, I would tell my father that she thought it was OK and vice versa. That way I usually got everything I wanted."

Some kid reading this might think that Neil was pretty lucky, but he would have liked his life to have more organization. "It was like being two people. At my dad's, I did my chores and rarely argued about what he asked me to do. At my mom's, I could be sloppy, play loud music, and eat what I wanted. But sometimes I messed up and started to behave at my dad's house like I did at mom's. That got me into trouble." Neil didn't find out who he really was until he left home for college and was able to put both sides of himself together without his parents' interference.

The Only Child as Surrogate Companion

Single parents may adultify their only child by involving him in their dating life and divorce issues. Parent and child spend so much time together and overcome so many obstacles that they can bond too closely. They may become best buddies who share secrets, and the role of the only child can evolve inappropriately into one of a surrogate companion.

Twenty-seven-year-old Zane was eight when his father left.

"One day, my father just didn't come home. He disappeared, and our money went with him. My mother was an artist, who did some freelance work, but it didn't bring in much. After Dad left, my mom was incredibly depressed, and it was my job to try to make her feel better. She told me that my dad had neglected her and was even abusive. I was crushed, because I adored my father, but I also wanted to protect my mother. It was hard for me to listen to all of that. In my mind, I became the man of the family right away. I helped out as much as a little kid could and went everywhere with my mother. If there was a social event, my mom took me with her, even when kids weren't exactly welcome. Believe it or not, my mom didn't have a date until I got to college. I was her date most of the time. So as a young kid, when I wanted to go out to play, I felt guilty, and in high school I felt disloyal having girlfriends."

Zane currently has a good job with an advertising agency and still talks to his mother every day. When they fight, it's like listening to an old married couple. Relationships with girls are challenging for Zane because he can't ever seem to leave the "friend zone" to establish a romance and let go of mom.

Fourteen-year-old Melanie and her mother, Joan, are the best of friends. Her parents divorced when Melanie was three, and they have always been the dynamic duo.

"I never really thought of Melanie as a child per se. She is the person I confide in after a day at work. When we needed more money, I ran ideas past Melanie. She is so creative that she helped me come up with an idea for a TV show about teen fashions that one of the cable networks just bought."

Melanie praises her mother's spontaneity and sense of fun. "Honestly," she says, "I have as good a time hanging out with my mom as I do with my friends." This year, however, Melanie started high school and wants to have more of a life apart from her mom. But Joan is holding on to her daughter like a kid with her teddy bear. If Melanie wants to spend the night at a friend's house, Joan asks, "Wouldn't you rather watch TV with me? I'll get a pizza, and we can sit around and laugh at the old shows on Nickelodeon."

Melanie doesn't want to disappoint the mother with whom she has been so close, so she stays home more than she likes. "My mother has given up so much for me," says Melanie. "How can I say no to her?" But if she doesn't start saying no, Melanie may share Zane's fate when she gets older and won't be able to establish her own identity.

Consequences of Adultifying an Only Child

We have seen that only children who take on adult roles can feel like outsiders among their peer group and may not be able to separate enough from their parents to establish fully independent lives. But as with perfectionism, this sin also has its positive aspects. But first, let's look at some of the negatives.

Negative Consequences

The only child who has too many adult responsibilities may never have a real childhood and may be cheated out of the spontaneity that is one of the hallmarks of being a kid.

When we allow our only child to make decisions that rightfully belong to adults, we hand over the keys to a kingdom that our little pretender to the throne isn't ready to govern. The confusion of being an adult in a child's body is bound to create distress once the euphoria of power has passed. That is what happened to Jacob Grossman.

"My parents were like immature teenagers," recalls fifty-five-year-old Jacob. "By the time I was ten, I realized that I would have to be the grown-up. My father was always working, and my mother suffered from hyperthyroidism, so her behavior was often bizarre. My parents fought all the time. My mother wanted me to be a child but also to take care of her. It was crazy. I was my mother's whole life, and I did everything to get away from that smothering."

Jacob's solution was to become as self-sufficient as possible. By the time he was fifteen, he made enough money mowing lawns to buy his mother a new sofa. "I built up a good business and didn't have to ask for much. I got to a place where my life wasn't dependent on my parents' happiness. Although things at home certainly weren't normal, I was not unloved."

But ultimately, growing up in a family where he needed to be the adult made Jacob somewhat insensitive to others. He thought everyone should be as competent as he. He relished being in control as a child, but as an adult he became frustrated when he discovered that he couldn't always be the officer in charge. He has had to work hard to be more tolerant of others and not to be so quick to ask more than people can give.

A child who is too much a part of the adult world may become a constant worrier and later on an adult who has difficulty being decisive.

A certain amount of adultifying is part and parcel of being an only child, because it's almost impossible to build an impenetrable wall between parents and child. Things slip out. Concerns for ailing relatives, money problems, conflicts at work, and the like can be kept from a child but only to a degree. Only children can't help hearing things because they are in the mix with their parents. One only child puts it this way, "Worrying is a method of control. If you worry about something enough, you can make sure that the outcome is what you want."

"I worry about everything," says twenty-three-year-old Nicky. "As an only child, I was included in most of the important decisions my parents made. When we bought a house, they wouldn't make a final decision until they knew that I was OK with it. That was a lot of pressure for me. What if the house turned out to be a dud? Then it would be my fault. My parents talked over everything with me, from getting a new coffeemaker to whether or not my mom should change jobs. I saw my parents put so much effort into everything that I think I should do the same. I don't know how to let go and wait to see what will happen. I'm always worried that I will make the wrong choices, and as I've gotten older, I realize that I don't trust my own instincts."

The child who becomes his parents' caretaker or a surrogate significant other for a single parent may always have to be the caretaker in adult relationships.

This child may find it difficult, if not impossible, to let someone else care for her, even when necessary. She may only be able to establish strong relationships with those who are needy. This is the situation for Darcy, who is unable to sustain friendships unless she acts as a mother.

Forty-two-year-old Leland takes the part of a father. "My dad passed away when I was fifteen, and my mother fell apart. She didn't know how to pay bills and had never had a job. I took over and had to show her how to do everything. I have been married and divorced twice to women who were extremely dependent, like my mother, but the relationships didn't work. Even my close friends rely on me to help them function. My best buddy is a recovering alcoholic, and I was the one who got him into rehab. I notice that I surround myself with people I have to take care of, and I have begun to dislike that role. Now I would like someone to take care of me, but I know that I will have trouble if I'm not sitting in the driver's seat."

The only child who is taken to Europe every summer, frequently eats at expensive gourmet restaurants, and stays with his parents at four-star resorts may not be able to adjust to life on his own without these privileges.

Twenty-nine-year-old Alice never thought there was anything to regret about being an only child, until recently, that is. Her job at a public relations firm in New York pays just enough for her to keep a very tiny roof over her head and some take-out from the local Chinese restaurant in her refrigerator. Her struggle to find a job and then to support living on her own in one of the world's most expensive cities has taught her that it will be a long time before she can enjoy even a semblance of the lifestyle her parents shared with her. She is discouraged by how slowly her career has advanced and by how little money she makes.

"If my parents had not taken me with them everywhere, I would never have known what I'm missing by not having access to great meals and fabulous resorts," she says. Most of my friends with siblings didn't get to go to those places with their parents. I feel disappointed in myself because I think I am going backward. I grew up with the life I should have now, so it's very frustrating. If I had siblings, I probably wouldn't expect so much so quickly."

Positive Consequences

The only child who shares in adult experiences and takes on more responsibilities than most kids may not always enjoy the status he is awarded. His position may even rob him of some childhood freedoms, but he may also gain considerably by being so wrapped up in the adult world. So if you have found yourself committing the sin of treating your child like an adult to one degree or another, as I certainly have, don't despair. Some good will come out of it.

Only children who have been given a measure of equality at home usually have a strong comfort level with adults. This can make job and school experiences more successful.

When twenty-three-year-old Sonia graduated from college two years ago, she started a tutoring business to support her acting career. "My parents have their own graphic-design firm," recounts Sonia, "and I used to watch them closely. They let me help in the office when I was growing up, so I had an idea of what it takes to run a business." Sonia was such a good observer that she learned to imitate how her parents talked with clients and handled problems. Her tutoring business took off right away, and now she makes more money than most of her friends from college who are working for corporations.

"They are amazed that I am my own boss and have done so well. Being an only child has been a huge advantage for me. Because I have been around adults so much, I can relate just as well to the parents of the kids I tutor as I can to their kids. I am able to talk with parents on their level, and they think I'm much older than twenty-three. Also, because I went so many places with my parents and met so many different kinds of people, I can get along with almost anyone, from the most conservative to the wackiest. If I weren't an only child, running a business like mine might be a lot harder."

A child who is well traveled and has been exposed to different cultures will be more capable of adjusting to new environments.

Jayce is a thirty-year-old investment banker and only child whose first job out of business school took him abroad. "The company that hired me wanted to know if I would take a position in Germany. I didn't speak the language and didn't know anyone there. But I had traveled extensively with my parents and felt that I could adapt quickly to a new country. So I packed up and left for Berlin. Everything turned out fine. Within a year, I knew enough German to get by fairly well, and I've made some good friends. It's been a great adventure."

Jayce is certain that if he had not been an only child whose parents started traveling with him when he was six months old, he might have passed on his company's offer. "I just don't think I would have been comfortable picking up and leaving unless my parents had made me such an important part of their lives."

Only children who are used to more adult responsibilities than kids with siblings may be less intimidated by the roles they have to assume when they grow up.

Parents who rely on their only child too much for emotional or physical support do their child a disservice on one level but may do them a service on another. Tasha is a thirty-one-year-old only child who has a six-year-old son. Like Darcy, she spent much of her childhood helping care for a parent with a disability.

"My mother was a single parent and had diabetes. So it was one thing after another. She relied on me so much that I became resentful, and as soon as I could, I moved away. But now that I am married and have a child of my own, I can see that helping my mom was the best training I could have had for motherhood. I know what it means to give up things for someone you love. I'm more patient with my son than my friends are with their kids."

An only child who has been part of decision-making processes with his parents knows what is involved in making thoughtful decisions.

Only children who have been too involved with adult concerns can grow up to be worriers, but they can also grow up to be wise souls, who comprehend what it means to make careful decisions. Louis, a twenty-five-year-old only child, has been thinking about changing jobs. He was offered a lot more money to leave his present position at a film studio in Los Angeles for a job working in marketing in another city.

"Most people would have jumped at the new job just for the money, but I had to look at every aspect of the deal and what it would mean in the long run. My parents often asked my opinion and took me seriously. They taught me to examine things thoroughly and ask good questions." Louis says that he sometimes "overthinks," but at least he understands that making good choices takes some care.

How Parents Can Avoid Adultifying Their Only Child

Here are a few important tips, culled from only-child parents with plenty of experience:

- Work on making your home a place where your kid can be a kid. In a kid-friendly home, a child feels free to bring his friends over, hang out, eat your food, and make a mess.

Relegate formality to special occasions or the living room. Make sure that there are enough places in your house where your child and his friends can unwind.

- Create boundaries. When you are tempted to make your child part of your marriage or involve him in marital conflicts, think again. Remember that your child loves you both equally and doesn't want to take sides.
- Don't give your child too much information about your relationship with your spouse or significant other. Your child only wants to know that you are there to guide and protect her.
- If you are a single parent, be especially careful not to make your child a confidante or bosom buddy. Don't give him particulars about your dates, other than to say something like, "We had a great dinner at Angeli."
- Definitely expose your child to cultural experiences, but don't make them mandatory or too intense. If your child can only enjoy a museum for fifteen minutes, leave after fifteen minutes. Take him to children's concerts and see how he reacts. Don't drag your seven-year-old, who would prefer an evening at home reading *Captain Underpants* to an evening of Beethoven, unless he is a budding musician who has insisted on attending.
- Children are not equipped to make adult decisions with you. Don't ask your nine-year-old child to give her opinion about whether or not grandma should go into a nursing home. Keep those kinds of decisions to yourself and explain them to her later in a way she can understand. If you are trying to choose a vacation spot, and your child begs to go to Disney World, but you want to go to Italy, you may decide as a family which one would be the most fun for everyone. But don't let your child dictate the choice alone.

Self-Test

Do You Treat Your Only Child like an Adult?

Test yourself and find out.

- Do you check in with your child about your marriage?
- Do you rely on your child to assume responsibilities that should only be undertaken by adults?
- Do you frequently take your child to adult events where she is usually the only person under thirty and must always be on her best behavior?
- Do you keep your child at home with you rather than setting up play dates because your only child is your best friend and you want to keep it that way?
- Do you fail to create meaningful boundaries between the adult world and your child's world? Do you tell your child "everything" because you think that it's best to be totally honest with children even though it may produce stress?
- Have you created a home that must always be in order and designer perfect?
- Do you depend on your child for your emotional well-being?
- Do you expect that your child can organize and prioritize as well as an adult?

If you answered yes to any of these questions, you may be adultifying your only child. Many parents adultify their only child intermittently. But the more conscious that parents are of this bad habit, the more quickly they can put a stop to it. Parents who try to mold their only child into a little adult are the same parents who may overpraise their child and give him a distorted view of himself. That is the seventh sin and the subject of the next chapter.

Chapter Seven

Overpraising

I am a thirty-seven-year-old only child with a wife and an only child of our own. Being an only child has had many benefits, but believe it or not, the difficult part was my parents' constant praising. According to them, I was good at everything, and they let me know it. No matter what I tried, no matter how well or poorly I did something, they told me that I was the best. I was a pretty bright kid, so underneath I knew better. My parents gave me a false sense of worth that I eventually had to overcome in school, at work, and with friends. It took years for me to get my bearings. I do things differently with my own child. I encourage and support him but save praise for when he really earns it. My parents' praise was meant to boost my self-esteem, but in fact it made me feel like an impostor.

Now we come to the seventh and final sin. Although it is the last of the series, it has a tremendous impact. Many parents of only children simply can't get enough of praising their kids, because that one child is the most wonderful, amazing creature in the universe. They have never and will never see anything like her again. In their desire to do the best for her, they try to bolster her psyche every chance they get. Whatever their child does even moderately well, no matter how small, is deserving of praise. Why? Because there is only one, and she is theirs to cuddle, coddle, and sustain.

Such parents may also be defensive about having just one child and may think that overpraising is a good way to compensate for not having other children. When they praise everything that seven-year-old Lila does, they may be trying to show the rest of the world that they are just as devoted parents as those with more than one. It goes along with thinking that having more than one child makes you more of a parent, which it doesn't.

Other factors can also lead to overpraising. Parents of only children who wait until they are in their thirties or forties to have a child may take the act of parenting more seriously than those who have their children in their twenties. Well traveled and with established careers, older parents often know more than younger parents about who they are. Having their child is the last frontier, and they intend to do it well. They have read all the books and are aware that building a child's confidence is a crucial part of doing a good job of parenting.

In my generation, most parents had not heard of self-esteem and had no idea of its importance. Most of the kids I knew, including me, only received praise when they did something absolutely fabulous. Fabulous might include saving the baby from choking, rescuing the family dog from an impending automobile accident, or getting straight A's. Otherwise we were expected to do our chores, behave ourselves, and respect family traditions. We didn't receive praise for doing what was required, only for doing what was exceptional. Somehow we made it through and transitioned into adulthood—with or without our self-esteem intact. Granted, I wouldn't have minded being fawned over for coming home with B's on my report card, but nothing doing. I would have been thrilled if my mother had praised me for washing all of the dishes after a huge Thanksgiving meal, but no one expected that I would do anything less. I was thanked nicely, but that was it.

In the sixties and seventies, my generation revolted. We were tired of being lumped together with parents who found nothing wrong with cultivating what we considered a herd mentality. We were revolutionaries who were going to be recognized for our uniqueness, but I don't recall hoping to raise my self-esteem (I didn't even know what that was) or worrying about whether anyone would even like what I was doing.

Today's only-child parents are the inheritors of that quest for individualism, which bred an intense interest in psychology and child development and about a million self-help books. Suddenly, how and what our children thought of themselves became crucial to their becoming productive members of society. Educators and psychologists told parents that high self-esteem was the way to guarantee a positive outcome for kids, and parents listened, particularly those with an only child. With only one child on whom to focus, many only-child parents have completely embraced the idea of self-esteem. But in the process, they have reduced the concept of true self-esteem—which ought to combine a strong sense of self-worth with the ability to handle challenges—to just making their child feel good by lavishing her with praise.

In families with siblings, many things that one child does may go unseen or unremarked upon, because parents are busy watching what another child is doing. Parents with multiple children don't have the time to pump up two or three kids' egos with elaborate praise twenty-four hours a day. But parents with one child can see and hear everything. The minute their child makes an observation like, "You know the ocean looks like the sky because they are both blue," he is congratulated as if he were a budding Ernest Hemingway, rather than just a normally observant child.

Only-child parents can be perfectionists with themselves as well as with their children, and many strive to be model parents. In their minds, the best parents do everything in their power to praise their child, thereby ensuring that he will grow up with high self-esteem. Deep down, they may be afraid that the critics who say that only children will grow up to be maladjusted are right. But they hope, if they can make their child "feel good" about himself, that this dire prediction will be avoided, and their child will mature into a wise adult. But praising, which is frequently offered in the form of compliments, and building self-esteem are actually quite different. One doesn't necessarily lead to the other. As with everything worthwhile, it's more complex than that.

Only-child parents may also be insecure because this is the first child they have raised. They may be unsure of how to guarantee a child's love and may be worried that if they do the wrong thing, the unthinkable could happen, and their child might not love them completely. What if their child feels slighted because they have failed to praise him enough? Parents with more than one child must spread attention around and usually don't worry about overlooking some small accomplishment. Only-child parents, however, may think that if they miss praising an especially good practice session on the piano or a supercharged run down a ski slope, their child will think that they don't care about him.

We are back to the magnifying-glass syndrome. Parents who worry that their only child will think that they are ignoring him might more profitably sort out how they can teach their child to compliment and reward himself instead of always turning to them for praise. But more about that later.

Praising an Only Child Too Much

Overpraising an only child can begin early. First-time parents, fascinated by their child, can barely turn away after each seemingly marvelous moment. They ooh and aah over everything their child learns, and each developmental plateau is a revelation. A baby's first smile, first time rolling over, first time sitting up, and first time walking are all events that merit full attention and unmitigated delight. But only-child parents may continue to praise every one of their child's achievements to the skies in general terms ("You are the most fabulous baby we have ever seen"), because this is not only the first time but also the only time that they will be watching an infant offspring's progress. But parents who continue praising their only child this way may raise an individual who expects that whatever he does, including throwing his squash against the wall, should be greeted with the same enthusiasm. "Wow, Ryder, you have the best throwing arm for a nine-month-old I've ever seen."

General Superlative Praise

This kind of praise has no perimeters and is not specific to what a child is actually doing at the moment. Of course, parents want their child to know they are proud of him and to back up his efforts, but general praise can lead a child to believe that everything he does may merit the same kind of over-the-top admiration.

"When we made the choice to have an only child, Bill and I knew that everything Kerry did would be special to us," says Marlene. "We were careful to record all the 'firsts' and praise Kerry when he learned something new. We didn't think there was anything wrong with telling him he could be the next Picasso. When he began playing baseball, he was a decent pitcher, who with some hard work should have been able to strike out a few batters. During his opening game, he did just that, and we could barely contain our praise. We told him that he was the best ballplayer in the world because we wanted to inspire him." But Kerry took their praise to heart, and after that initial game he strutted around thinking that he was a star. In reality, he wasn't able to duplicate his initial success and spent much of the season on the bench, angry at the coach and confused. If he was as good as his parents told him he was, why wasn't he playing?

Praise should send an only child the message that he is loved and accepted for the person he is, not for the person his parents hope he will become. Kids like Kerry are set up for failure and disappointment, because merely stroking them doesn't address their real strengths or help them improve their weaknesses. General praise may lead an only child to think that no one is better than he, no one more special, no one more deserving. That's a dangerous precedent to set.

Zelda is a twelve-year-old only child whose parents have doted on her since she was born. They tried for years to have a child, so when she came along, she was their godsend, their superstar. Zelda's parents tried to convince her that she was the most talented at whatever she attempted.

"We felt that praising Zelda would help her achieve what she wanted. And of course, since she is our only child, we want her to have everything. Last year, she took up tennis, and from the beginning we told her that she was great. Her father and I felt it was important for her to hear this so that she would feel that she was on the same level with the other kids, some of whom are older than she. But it backfired. The more we complimented Zelda, the less enthusiastic she was about tennis. In fact, one day she was so upset about going to the courts that she began crying in the car and wanted to give up altogether. When I asked what was wrong, she said, 'Mom, you lied to me. I'm not the best player and everybody knows it. Why do you tell me those things? I feel like I can't be as good as you think I am.'"

Zelda's parents weren't deliberately trying to mislead her, but they didn't know another way to encourage her efforts. They could have told Zelda how much her serve or backhand had improved and pointed out specific strategies she had used to achieve a good result. Then they could have told her how proud her determination made them. That way, Zelda would have felt encouraged and validated. She would have respected her own efforts and known that they had been acknowledged. Her parents' general "greats" exposed Zelda's natural insecurities instead of making her feel competent about her performance in tennis.

Feeling Good Isn't the Same as Having Self-Esteem

So much of what happens in our culture is aimed at making us feel good. Buying a new car will make us feel good. Wearing the latest fashions will make us feel good. So who doesn't want to feel good? But these external fixes last for only a short time. Three months after getting our new car, there are shopping cart dings in the door, and we are angry and not feeling so good anymore. Once we have worn the new clothes a few times, we find as much fault with them as we did with our old clothes. In order for us to make our only children (or ourselves) feel good, we have to build self-esteem step-by-step. Merely heaping acclaim on a child doesn't build true self-worth and genuine confidence. Parents need to create an environment in which their only child will feel capable of overcoming obstacles and knowing themselves, flaws and all. An only child who has been overpraised may not be able to distinguish between feeling good and feeling able.

Bonnie, an only child and a senior in high school, went on a "bonding" trip with her class and discovered that when she had to meet a challenge head on without her parents, she froze. In the past, her parents had always been there to praise her and tell her that she was fabulous. Part of the bonding experience included a ropes course, which terrified Bonnie.

"I stood at the bottom of the course, looking up at the rope walkway, which was only two inches wide, and I was sure that I would never be able to get up there. Until that day, any challenges I had to meet seemed possible because my parents were always around to tell me how great I was or how amazing I would be—whether it was applying to college, editing the school newspaper, or being the captain of the volleyball team. But for the first time, they weren't there to compliment me, and I needed to hear their words. So as I was standing in line to climb the course, I got sick to my stomach and couldn't do it. The other kids tried to help me, but I just had no faith in myself."

Bonnie was the only kid in her class who came home without testing herself. While the other kids were full of pride, Bonnie couldn't help thinking that she was a loser. While the other kids were patting themselves on the back for having overcome fears, Bonnie's fears were still alive and well. Bonnie's parents thought that they had given her strong self-esteem, but when she had to draw on that self-esteem to take a risk, she couldn't do it, because validation always came from someone else. Bonnie had never developed a sense of what she really could do. It was all about what her adoring parents thought she could do.

Haunted by stereotypes of only children as misfits, parents may think that they have to go to extremes to boost their child's ego. They can also be terrified that their child will turn out to be contentedly average, which can be a letdown when you know there won't be any more kids on the way. Parents of only children may say that they "just want our kid to be happy," but truthfully, they yearn for more than that. They hope that their child will distinguish himself in some way. Fearing that their child may not excel, some parents will overpraise, trying to ensure the outcome they want: high achievement.

Twenty-five-year-old Yuval, an only child of two older parents, never had a day when his mother or father didn't tell him he was amazing. They both had a number of siblings, and when they realized that they were not going to have more children, their families were appalled. They were of the opinion that only children are strange and incapable of handling life. Determined to avoid this fate, Yuval's parents believed that acres of praise would make their child so confident that he would be able to do anything. If he did the chores that any other sixteen-year-old was expected to do, his mother gave him five extra dollars in his allowance. When he did his homework neatly and on time, they never said, "You tackled a hard problem and solved it. Well done." What they said was, "You are a fantastic mathematician." When he cleaned his room after weeks of using it as a trash heap, his mother didn't say, "I really appreciate the way you put away your clothes." What she said was, "You have done such a great job, you could open your own cleaning business." His whole life was long on compliments and short on actual self-assuredness. He was praised for everything, but after a while it all became background noise, something he expected to be there but nothing he wanted to think about.

Things changed when Yuval graduated from college and got his first job in publishing. "All of a sudden, I was expected to do what I considered to be mindless busywork and got no rewards for it. No one told me that I was amazing. No one said that I was so good that I was bound to become president of the company. I had to learn the job from the ground up, and I couldn't figure out why my supervisor wasn't showering me with praise. After a year, I wanted to quit, because I couldn't see the point of working hard without being verbally rewarded." Yuval hungered for constant reinforcement, but it took a few years in therapy for him to realize that he didn't really understand praise because he couldn't praise himself. He never had to because his parents had always done it for him. They didn't give him the room to figure out what pleased *him* about his accomplishments and what disappointed *him*. They were too busy shoring him up with empty compliments. If Yuval had learned to satisfy himself, he wouldn't have had to look to others for satisfaction.

Making Up for Lost Time

When both parents work and come home to their only child at the end of the day, they are anxious to connect and show her how significant she is to them, because they have not been with her all day. This child is their whole world, and having been gone, they may feel compelled to let her know that she is important to them in every way. Because parents aren't there during the day to praise, they try to make up for it in the evening or on weekends by complimenting everything their child does. If a single parent works full-time, she may feel particularly driven to bestow praise. It's a form of overcompensation that at first glance seems benign and perhaps even necessary to a child's well-being. But a parent who is frequently at home with a child can praise small things throughout the day in a much more meaningful (because it's specific) way.

Sandi is five years old. Her mother works part-time while Sandi is in school. After Sandi's mother picks up her daughter at 3:00, they go home and settle in. Sandi's mom often likes to get the laundry done before dinner. Sandi helps fold and put it away. When she does a good job, her mother tells her, "Thanks for folding the towels so neatly; it was a big help." Sandi also likes to practice printing her letters while her mom works on the computer. She can see what Sandi is doing and can praise her daughter's work as it improves. "Sandi, I'm impressed. Your letters are so neat, and you have done a great job with the B. You had a hard time with that last week, but now it looks like you've got it down."

Parents who come home tired after work may not have the patience to use the kind of descriptive praise that focuses on specifics. Their child may bombard them with examples of what he has done at school or at home with the babysitter or housekeeper while they were gone.

"Dad, look at the painting I made of sharks for science. What do you think?" Dad's response could very likely be, "That's fantastic. You are an amazing artist," instead of, "You really captured what a shark's body looks like, and the teeth you drew look so sharp, they scare me." Dad feels guilty and thinks that telling his son that he is the best will assure him that his dad's love is strong and ever present.

Or mom may come home to her six-year-old, who has just dressed her Barbies in toilet paper and say, "Justine, you are the best fashion designer in the world." Then as the evening progresses, everything else that Justine does may receive the same kind of praise. Her drawing of the family cat is "spectacular," and she set the table like a "professional." Meanwhile, Justine takes all of this in but can't figure out how she got to be so good at all of these things. What did she really do to deserve her mother's accolades? "When I get home after work," says Pearl, Justine's mother, "I want my only child to know how much I love and admire her. So I compliment her as much as possible. I feel terrible that I'm not around to see all the little things she does during the day. I want Justine to know how much I love her. On weekends, we spend a lot of time together, and when she does something cute or picks up her toys without my asking, I don't mind telling her how wonderful she is."

But Pearl might mind if she knew that generic praise is not the way to build her child's self-esteem. Even if she feels guilty about leaving Justine during the day, she should make an effort to praise her daughter in specific ways, the way Sandi is praised. If she does, Justine will come to understand that when she does something well, it is because she personally took the steps to get there. Pearl needs to understand that love and praise are not one and the same. Compliments are cheap and easy. Pearl has not taken the time to recognize how Justine has progressed from drawing rudimentary stick figures to drawing figures with clothes and facial expressions. A child who knows how she got to where she was going is a child who can learn to make connections, think independently, and function competently, because she believes in herself and her own abilities.

Common Ways to Overpraise

Although each parent is unique and endlessly inventive in the ways she overpraises her child, there are several general types of overpraising that we all have engaged in.

Using Physical Affection as Praise

Who can resist cuddling, kissing, and hugging their only child? This is a parent's greatest love, the darling who gives life purpose and meaning. But physical affection given merely as praise should be limited. Children who are hugged and kissed whenever they do something good may begin to do things in order to get that praise, instead of doing things to please themselves. Parents of only children are so physically and mentally attached to their "baby" that physical affection can become a way to say, "We adore you and you're terrific" (all the time). So what's wrong with that? It can lead an only child to become so totally dependent on physical affection for validation that he expects to be treated that way by everyone all of his life. Or it can create a child who can't understand when it's appropriate to be physically affectionate. He wants it all the time because it feels good. Constant physical praise, paired with verbal praise, can also result in a child who is preoccupied with pleasing. Of course, being spontaneously affectionate with a child is crucial to his healthy development. But I am talking about parents who use excessive expressions of physical praise, which can confuse a child and stunt his ability to look to himself for confidence.

Take Meg and her husband, Willis, for instance. They are the parents of an only child, Cody, who is twelve. Both Meg and Willis grew up in large families where physical affection was at a minimum. Praise was generally verbal and was intermittent. They got the usual good-night kisses and hugs, but it wasn't enough to be satisfying. When they had Cody, they wanted to do things differently and swore that he would receive as much hugging and cuddling as they could provide. In fact, they chose to have an only child so that they could give Cody the kind of attention that they didn't receive growing up in large families.

"As soon as Cody was old enough to understand the connection between doing something well and hugs and kisses, we made sure to respond to good behavior or good work with physical affection. If he scored a goal in soccer, we gave him lots of hugs when he came over to the sideline. When he brought home a good grade on a math test, we not only told him how exceptional he was, we also loaded him up with big hugs and lots of kisses. When he got older, he started to expect that kind of reaction from us no matter what.

"A few months ago, my mother became ill, and we were preoccupied with her needs. We had her move in with us for a few months so that it would be easier to care for her. My siblings live far away, and all of my mother's doctors are here. Our ability to focus entirely on Cody was disrupted and household routines changed. I noticed that he became increasingly dependent on us for physical affection. He would literally hang on us and get upset if we didn't recognize something he had done with physical acknowledgment.

"One day, he brought home an A on a social studies project and expected that we would immediately respond with bear hugs. But I was on my way to take my mother to the doctor, and his dad was busy trying to sort out my mother's Medicare paperwork. Cody started to cry and whimpered, 'Don't I get a hug for what I did?' I had to drop everything to console him and was late for my mother's appointment. He would even become jealous when I showed my mother affection. Cody would try to get between us, and although he was never cruel to my mom, he certainly wanted to make sure that he got his share of physical love. Why couldn't he wait?"

Cody couldn't wait because his comfort zone had been invaded. He was so used to being rewarded with physical affection that he had no idea of how to give himself a big hug when others couldn't.

Essentially, Cody temporarily reverted to being a baby, waiting for others to gratify him.

When an only child grows up and establishes romantic relationships, the need for physical praise can interfere with a couple's relationship rather than bringing them closer together. This is what happened to Larissa, a twenty-eight-year-old only child. She has been in two serious relationships since college, both of which ended because Larissa demanded so much physical praise from her boyfriends.

"I was brought up by two devoted parents, who lavished me with physical love. I was given kisses and hugs for anything I did that my parents thought was good. If I set the table correctly, my father would plant a kiss on my head, and if I did my chores without a fuss, my mother would squeeze the life out of me. I ate it all up even though I wasn't always too clear about why they were so demonstrative. Usually, the things I did seemed pretty ordinary to me. The problem was that I came to rely on them to praise me that way all the time, and if for some reason they didn't, I had a fit.

"I would say, 'You didn't give me a kiss. Don't you like my drawing?' Then when I had a serious boyfriend, I wanted him to do the same on a regular basis. He was probably no different than a lot of men, but I expected more. In fact, I expected a kiss or hug, or compliment, whenever I did something for him, like make dinner or pick up the tickets for a movie. 'Thank you' or 'You're so sweet' weren't enough for me. I wanted the whole enchilada. What I wanted was my parents, and it drove him away from me. I was too demanding. Then I did the same thing with my next boyfriend, who was more physically demonstrative but had his limits as well. I thought there was something wrong with them, but now I know that it's my problem, and if I want to have a lasting relationship with a man, I have to learn how to reward myself rather than always relying on others for strokes."

An only child who receives appropriate physical and verbal praise and appropriate spontaneous affection (for no particular reason) while growing up will be secure enough to know that every kind act or every responsibility fulfilled doesn't require physical praise to be honored. The honor lies in doing something from the heart.

Putting Your Child on a Pedestal

Then there is the child who, after being praised without reservation, can begin to believe that he is godlike and can do no wrong. His parents told him so often that he was exceptional and better than others that he now believes it wholly. These are children who stand the chance of growing up into narcissistic adults for whom consequences and the feelings of others are of little interest. They live for themselves because their parents designed it that way. All they heard throughout their lives was, "You're fabulous." "You're great." Never a discouraging word.

Jay, a fifty-six-year-old only child, grew up the beloved son of a wealthy New York businessman. He was a brilliant student and attended the best schools in the city. His mother and father idolized him and rarely, if ever, found fault with him.

Looking back, Jay says, "I don't think that my parents ever told me that they didn't approve of something I had done. I was their golden boy, who became a cocky young adult. My parents' praise and compliments gave me an enormous ego. So I thought that I could do just about anything without being caught. In graduate school, I got tired of relying on them financially, so a friend and I started a ski theft ring in Colorado, where I was going to school. It was easy money and exciting. We got away with it by the skin of our teeth. When we left Vail, the cops were beginning to catch on. But making an escape only made me feel more invincible, and I led the rest of my life that way, until I was arrested for selling marijuana when I was in my thirties and again for shady real estate deals in my forties.

"I cheated on my wife and my business partners because I thought I could get away with that too. Both my marriage and business fell apart, and I've had to rethink everything my parents told me. It's taken me a long time to turn myself into someone who doesn't think he is above the law and is even somewhat responsive to other people's needs."

Jay was a soul in torment. His parents thought that they were giving him the best possible start in life, but they were actually setting him up for a huge fall.

Essentially the same thing happened to Wesley, a twenty-six-year-old only child of Chinese immigrants. Wesley's parents worshipped at the shrine of Wesley. He was the only one who could carry on the family name, and it was expected that he would succeed—at something important. When Wesley was six, his parents gave him violin lessons. He showed great promise from the beginning, and his parents fawned over him. As long as he practiced and played well, he was the prince who could do no wrong. When he was in his early teens, Wesley began winning regional, state, and national competitions. But after a while, he stopped practicing the four hours a day needed to sustain top-level performance.

"My parents gave me such an inflated sense of my talent that I thought I could become the next Itzhak Perlman without breaking a sweat. Well, that didn't work, and instead of playing with the New York Philharmonic, I wound up at junior college taking courses to get into a decent university. I blew what could have been a promising career and had to find something else to do. My ego got in the way of being successful. In Chinese culture, an only boy child is revered as if he were a king. That's not good, since kings don't have to do much for themselves or face many consequences."

Unfortunately, neither Jay nor Wesley benefited from their parents' adulation. If only their parents had someone to tell them that inflating an only child's ego puts him on the road to failure, not on the path to good fortune.

Praising with Material Rewards

Parents who reward their only child's good behavior or good performance with material gifts teach their child that doing a good job equals, "I deserve something" instead of, "I'm proud of myself." There is a difference between overindulgence and using material things as praise.

The parent who overindulges a child usually does so spontaneously and without a specific purpose. Or they may overindulge because they don't know how to do anything else. But when a child is given a Tiffany bracelet for getting an A on a history paper, or when parents hand out cookies each time a child does a required chore, a deliberate message is being sent. The child who is only motivated to do well in order to receive gifts is not doing anything for himself. The satisfaction he derives from the cookie or the newest remote-controlled car is transitory. He knows what tricks to perform to get what he wants. Everything becomes a means to an end, so the child doesn't comprehend that learning is about trial and error and is a responsibility. Learning often means starting at the bottom and reaching for the top. If a child achieves just because daddy is going to buy her something shiny, she can't know how far she can go under her own steam.

Holding back material praise with only children is crucial because, to begin with, only-child parents tend to give more to one child than they would if they had two. Then if parents add consistent material praise, an adorable little princess can quickly become a little tyrant, who expects gifts for every toy put away and every homework assignment completed.

Twelve-year-old Missy is one of those children. Her parents started rewarding her with gifts and cash as soon as she began asking why she had to do homework. Her parents' response was, "because your teacher wants you to and because it helps you learn." This wasn't good enough for her. She whined and complained every night, and because she was her parents' only child and their treasure, they figured that there was no harm in some bribery to get her going. "We told her that if she turned all of her homework in for the week and did well on quizzes, we would give her money to go to the mall and buy whatever she wanted. Although we aren't rich, we felt that we could stretch ourselves because we had only one. We hoped that the rewards would lead her to get better grades and would drive her to be proud of herself. We had no idea that our plan to inspire her would make her so greedy that we would end up literally paying her to do homework." Missy got so used to getting money and presents from her parents for doing well that one day she turned to them and said outright, "Mom, if I do my English homework, can I have a new pair of Pumas?"

Missy's parents realized that they had created a monster. "We tried to explain to her that the money and gifts were a reward for a job well done and weren't to be expected." But Missy didn't get it, and withdrawal was painful for everybody. Missy's parents had to cut her off cold turkey in order to set her straight and save their bank account, which was rapidly dwindling because Missy had been so responsive to their bribes. Missy's only motivation for doing well in school became trips to the mall, iPods, and so forth. For Missy's friends, getting good grades was a reward in itself, but not for her.

There is a difference between giving presents for birthdays, Christmas, or Hanukkah and giving presents as recurring rewards for doing what is legitimately expected. There is nothing wrong with the occasional "this is because we love you" gift, with the emphasis on the occasional. Kids who have been praised too often with material things can't work toward a goal without feeling that they deserve something for every ounce of energy expended.

Consequences of Overpraising an Only Child

Overpraising a child can create unrealistic expectations.

An only child who is overpraised can become an approval addict, who will do almost anything for praise.

Parents who praise their only child for merely getting out of bed in the morning and breathing may raise a child who becomes an approval addict. This fixated child will do almost anything for praise and can do little without it. He may drive his teachers crazy because he requires constant reinforcement, and he may even cheat to get the approval he requires. Eleven-year-old Jamal is such a child. "We wanted Jamal to do well in school," says Jamal's mother, Libby. "Since he is our only child, we are committed to helping him become someone special." But recently, Jamal bitterly disappointed his parents. They were called into school because his teacher caught Jamal cheating on a math test. Libby and her husband, George, were shocked. Those weren't the values they had taught their son. Instead of telling his parents that he was having trouble with math, Jamal lost perspective and decided to cheat. He simply couldn't stand the thought of bringing home a poor grade and making his parents unhappy. Jamal also hangs around the teacher's desk and wants her approval for every sentence he writes and every math problem he solves. In their last teacher conference, Jamal's parents were surprised to hear that their son felt so unsteady, as they had invested so much in making him feel secure.

Overpraising may result in a child who expects positive reinforcement for everything she does, even when it's mediocre.

Parents who overpraise their only child may raise a person whose judgment about herself is flawed. The child whose parents consider her every effort brilliant may not be able to distinguish between what is mediocre and what is splendid.

Serena is a junior in high school and is having difficulty with her English teacher. "I've enjoyed being an only child, because my parents really care about what I do. They read my papers for school and think that I am a great writer. But this year, I have a teacher who doesn't like what I do. She tells me that I have to focus more on developing my ideas and that I don't support them thoroughly enough. But I think my writing is fine and so do my parents. My teacher just doesn't like me." Serena's teacher likes her well enough, but Serena has been raised to believe that everything she does is above average, even when it isn't. But no matter, she still expects praise, because her parents have *taught* her to expect it.

The child who is overpraised may think that doing something that is mediocre is the same as doing something that is her best. Serena already "knows" that she is an accomplished writer because her parents have made her feel like one. So she doesn't think there is any reason for her to work as hard as her teacher asks her to, at least until her final grades come in.

Overpraising can create pressure that backfires.

I have never met a parent of an only child who doesn't believe that her child is fantastic. When you have just one, it's almost impossible not to think that. But that's a lot for one person to live up to. No one can be the best all the time, and the child who feels that he must be spectacular because his parents already think it is so is living on the edge. There will be times when a child doesn't do his best or has to back off because the pressure is too great. When parents see this happening, they need to rethink what they expect from their child and take a fresh look at how in touch they are with the person they love most in the world.

Inappropriate praise can lead to an only child becoming an outsider with other kids. The child who claims supremacy at school because he is supreme at home may find himself confronting some peers who don't welcome him.

When Kurt left elementary school for middle school, he had a difficult time making new friends. He found himself jostling for position. He thought he was pretty cool because his parents never let him forget that he was special. So instead of waiting and letting the kids he wanted to be friends with come to him, he aggressively courted them. Kurt tried to ingratiate himself with one group after another. He would sit with kids at lunch and brag about what a good basketball player he was and how well he did in math. But the reaction he got wasn't what he expected. The more he talked about himself and tried to get other kids involved in plans to get together or play ball, the more quickly they moved away from him. Kurt spent much of the first year at his new school being excluded. Finally, one of the kids laid into him. Who did he think he was always talking about himself and acting like he was king of the hill? Why did he think that they would want to do anything with him? Once Kurt heard the truth from other kids, he gained some humility and found a close group of friends. He finally listened to other kids and let them take the lead in suggesting activities, which helped him discover that being cooperative can be more fun than being bossy.

Overpraising can create a distorted idea of approval.

The child who is praised too much will have difficulty rewarding herself and may always have to look to others for approval. As we have seen earlier in this chapter, this contributes little to strong self-esteem. The child who is praised for what he has not earned can't feel his own pulse. This is a child who may be afraid to try because he's afraid he might fail. Like Yuval, he will always be looking over his shoulder for adult approval, and when it isn't there, he will want to move on or give up rather than find a solution.

If a child is overpraised, he may grow up thinking that he is only loved when he is praised. Unconditional love that comes without strings or attachments may be foreign to him. He may not understand what all children should know in their gut: that love does not always have to include verbal or physical praise. Love can be communicated through a smile, a fleeting touch, a tone of voice, and words of encouragement. It isn't always about being the "best" or the "most" anything.

An inflated sense of self-worth that is the product of overpraising can isolate an only child from the very friends who could help him learn what siblings teach one another: tolerance, conflict resolution, and relationship maintenance. Kurt's friendships, for instance, are essential to his growing up as an emotionally balanced only child who cares for others and doesn't think that he knows more than everyone else does.

One of our most important jobs as parents is to help our only children build healthy self-esteem. Unquestionably, most only children receive more than their share of attention from parents. The praise that parents give their child for learning to master a task or doing something to the best of his ability should not be opportunities for lavishing even more attention, but rather a way to make a child feel secure about who he is and about what his talents are.

Because only children are usually so close to their parents and can be overly sheltered by them, it's critical for parents to differentiate between veneration and effective praise.

This is no small order and certainly doesn't mean that you shouldn't put your arms around your cherished only child and tell her how wonderful she is. But that kind of approbation should never be all a child hears. Home is a place where child and parents should be able to share experiences and draw strength from one another, a place where people know you for better or worse. Parents who understand that healthy self-esteem is a combination of feeling loved and capable will raise a child who expects the best from himself.

Benefits of Appropriate Praise

Although you can offer your only child too much inappropriate praise, it's hard to give too much of the right kind of praise. Some benefits of that praise are as follows:

- Only children with a realistic sense of self-worth will have an easier time socially. The only child whose parents have always told him that he is "the best" will have difficulty interacting with other kids because he will want to steal the show.
- Children with authentic self-esteem, who can take responsibility for their actions, tend to have a positive influence on others and are more accepting of change.
- Children who are praised specifically for what they do well or what they try hard to achieve will not feel entitled to everything or appear overly confident on the outside while feeling insecure on the inside.

How Parents Can Avoid Overpraising Their Only Child

These strategies will help you moderate the overpraising habit:

- When discussing your child's accomplishments, avoid superlatives. Make the language of praise specific and descriptive.

- Offer constructive criticism along with specific praise. This will make your child more secure with her strengths and help her identify what she needs to improve.
- When your child tries something that is difficult, encourage her with words like, "Do your best, and don't be afraid if it doesn't work out. You can always try again." But saying, "Of course, you can do it" doesn't tell her that you fully understand the elements involved in doing something tough. You are more likely to overwhelm her with pressure rather than giving her the confidence she needs.
- Give your child the opportunity to work out disagreements with friends on his own, unless behavior gets physical. Praise your child when he is able to compromise with friends and let them take the lead as well as being a leader himself. A child who feels superior to other kids will find few friends.
- It's your only child's responsibility to do well in school. Don't reward him for every assignment completed. Offer occasional rewards for improvement that will give him a boost but will not lead to unrealistic expectations.

Self-Test

Are You an Overpraising Parent?

Test yourself and find out.

- Do you find yourself regularly using superlatives when you praise your child? For example, do you say things like the following: "You are the prettiest girl in the world." "You are the most amazing basketball player. You're bound to be the next Shaquille O'Neal."

- Is your child disappointed when others don't praise him with the same enthusiasm he receives at home?
- Do you think that every day is another chance for you to make your child feel good? Do you confuse that with building self-esteem?
- Do you notice that your child adopts an overly confident manner when faced with new or somewhat uncomfortable situations?
- Do you equate complimenting your child with loving him?

If you answered yes to any of these questions, chances are that you overpraise your only child. Of course, the right kind of praise is essential and constructive, but the wrong kind of praise can have negative consequences.

Epilogue

Having an only child is a unique and joyful experience that brings many rewards and presents many interesting challenges. The sins that I have discussed in this book will do no great harm unless they are habitual and parents fail to see how they will play out with their child in the real world.

As I mentioned at the beginning of this journey, I have committed all of these sins in some form, to some extent. I was fortunate because someone or something saved me from committing them without limit. Sometimes one of my daughter's teachers, sometimes a friend, sometimes my husband, and sometimes even my child herself brought me back to my senses. But if I had known what the seven sins were, I would have taken measures to avoid them.

But I was lucky and so are you. Now that you have an idea of what to look for, you can monitor yourself and ask others for help as well. You won't let the sins steal what you prize most in the world: raising your only child to become a happy, confident person, who can take risks, withstand failures, relish success, and best of all know that he is loved for who he is.

Notes

Introduction

1. I. Caesar and V. Youmans, "Tea for Two," 1924.

Chapter One

1. C. Whitham, *The Answer Is No* (Los Angeles: Perspective, 1994), 20.
2. W. Mogel, *The Blessing of a Skinned Knee: Using Jewish Teachings to Raise Self-Reliant Children* (New York: Penguin USA, 2001), 70.
3. Whitham, 58–62.

Chapter Two

1. Bureau of Justice Statistics, U.S. Department of Justice [http://www.ojp.usdoj.gov]. Feb. 2004.
2. D. Goleman, *Emotional Intelligence: Why It Can Matter More Than IQ* (New York: Bantam Books, 1995), 222.
3. Goleman, *Emotional Intelligence*, 223.
4. C. Pickhardt, *Keys to Parenting the Only Child* (Hauppauge, N.Y.: Barrons, 1997), 34.
5. Ibid.

Chapter Three

1. S. Newman, *Parenting an Only Child: The Joys and Challenges of Raising Your One and Only* (New York: Broadway Books, 2001), 101.

2. D. Kindlon, *Too Much of a Good Thing: Raising Children of Character in an Indulgent Age* (New York: Miramax, 2003), 4.
3. Newman, 125.
4. N. Asher, "The Only Child Dilemma." *Only Child*, 1998, *2*(3), 27–29.

Chapter Five

1. Pickhardt, 64.

Resources

I have found the following books to be both practical and inspiring. They are excellent resources for parents of only children who strive to avoid the seven sins.

Coles, R. *The Moral Intelligence of Children: How to Raise a Moral Child.* New York: Random House, 1997.

Goleman, D. *Emotional Intelligence: Why It Can Matter More Than IQ.* New York: Bantam Books, 1995.

Hallowell, E., and Thompson, M. *Finding the Heart of the Child: Essays on Children, Families, and Schools.* Washington, D.C.: National Association of Independent Schools, 1993.

McGrath, E. *My One and Only: The Special Experience of the Only Child.* New York: Morrow, 1989.

Nachman, P., with Thompson, A. *You and Your Only Child: The Joys, Myths, and Challenges of Raising an Only Child.* New York: HarperCollins, 1997.

Newman, S. *Parenting an Only Child: The Joys and Challenges of Raising Your One and Only.* New York: Broadway Books, 2001.

Pickhardt, C. *Keys to Parenting the Only Child.* Hauppauge, N.Y.: Barrons, 1997.

Sifford, D. *The Only Child: Being One, Loving One, Understanding One, Raising One.* New York: HarperCollins, 1986.

About the Author

Although she has been an educator and writer for most of her life, Carolyn White considers raising her child the most important job she has ever had. She agrees with the late Jacqueline Kennedy, who felt that if you are not successful with your children, little else in life matters. Twenty-three years ago, when she and her husband Charles had their daughter, they had no idea that their roles as parents of an only child would ultimately inspire them to connect with other parents of only children throughout the world.

For the past seven years, White has been the editor in chief of *Only Child*, a publication for only children of all ages and for their parents, relatives, and friends. She has interviewed hundreds of only children and has provided advice to thousands of them and their parents, from the United States and Europe to India and China. In fact, she is often called the *Dear Abby* of only children. Her many articles for *Only Child* have covered everything from the relationships between single parents and their only children to helping adult only children find geriatric-care managers for elderly parents.

White received her bachelor's degree from Goddard College and did her graduate work at the University of Massachusetts; Wesleyan University in Middletown, Connecticut; and the University of California-Los Angeles. She taught English and journalism to high school students for ten years, was a college counselor, and for the past six years has been an assistant director of admissions at Crossroads School (a private school for grades K–12) in Santa Monica, California. In her capacity as an admissions director, she has the opportunity to meet with hundreds of only children and their parents and confer with them about parenting, education, and life choices.

The Seven Common Sins of Parenting an Only Child is the culmination of years of experience raising an only child and advising only children and their parents about how to have the most rewarding only-child experience.